Trout Farming in the People's Republic of Boulder

And Other True Tails

Peggy Ewegen Cline

Trout Farming in the People's Republic of Boulder
And Other True Tails
Peggy Ewegen Cline
Mountain Motivation

Published by Mountain Motivation, Erie, CO

Cover and Interior design: Davis Creative Publishing,
    DavisCreativePublishing.com
Cover Illustration: Kristen Olsen, Genesee, CO

Library of Congress Cataloging-in-Publication Data
(Provided by Cassidy Cataloguing Services, Inc.)

Names: Cline, Peggy Ewegen, author.
Title: Trout farming in the People's Republic of Boulder, and other true tails / Peggy Ewegen Cline.
Description: Erie, CO : Mountain Motivation, [2024] | Includes bibliographical references.
Identifiers: ISBN: 979-8-9903904-0-9 (paperback) | 979-8-9903904-1-6 (ebook) | LCCN: 2024907409
Subjects: LCSH: Trout farming--Colorado--Boulder. | Pets--Behavior. | Students. | Coming of age. | BISAC: BIOGRAPHY & AUTOBIOGRAPHY / Memoirs. | NATURE / Animals / General. | YOUNG ADULT FICTION / Coming of Age.
Classification: LCC: PS3603.L5546 T76 2024 | DDC: 818/.6--dc23

Dedication

I wish to dedicate Trout Farming in the People's Republic of Boulder to my late husband, Steven Cline and his father, Kenneth Cline, Sr. Steve is shown on the cover, posing in one and hiding from Boulder Daily Camera reporters in the other! Steve and his father took trout farming and fish delivery to customers to a high level of care and respect. They believed in the humane delivery of live trout and customer satisfaction with a few extra fish added for their gratitude to each customer.

My dedication also deservedly belongs to my parents, John and Marie Ewegen whose intelligent farming methods and dedicated homemaking skills made life on the farm a successfully healthy, safe and interactive life.

Table of Contents

Trout Farming in the People's Republic of Boulder

Sapillo, New Mexico

One of the privileges of owning a trout farm was that of our journeys into amazingly beautiful places that most people were never allowed to see.

Back in the days before New Mexico closed its borders to Colorado fish for fear of whirling disease, gill disease, ick, fluky livers, reduced slime and maybe the heartbreak of psoriasis, Sapillo, New Mexico, was a memorable trout delivery.

As we entered the little village of Sapillo, the small grocery store beckoned for a cultural experience. The unfinished wood floor squeaked as we entered to blend in with the English spoken softly with Spanish accents. Dark wooden shelves were filled with a variety of sundries that could keep a person supplied for weeks as they journeyed farther into the interior. One could even buy a hat that proudly displayed, "Sapillo Market" where "Who Farted?" might have been.

The little houses leading up to the hacienda where we were to unload our fish were not humbled by the presence of the immense home, but were more of a tribute. The earth-toned and Mexican pink adobe and particle board-sided huts surrounded by brush were undaunted, even with the rusted automobiles that collected beside them. Pots of geraniums in some yards glowed proudly among the other collections of unused metal and colorful plastic. Simple and lacking the wealth of some of their neighbors, yet not poverty-stricken, the homes seemed to emit an aura of a lifestyle that had been selected, not forced upon them. They bespoke simpler times, where they were securely and happily settled into their own little time warp where the haste and bustle of our fish deliveries seemed almost grossly out of place.

The hacienda surrounded a plaza where we were graciously greeted by one of the owners- a thirty-year-old Texan woman, which caused us to wonder what she had done to deserve such a spread of land and home.

"Hello, Mr. and Mrs. Clii-ine. Would you like something to drink?" I liked that whenever we delivered to Texans in New Mexico, even though we were always younger than the owners, we were called Mr. and Mrs. Cline, drawn out to three syllables.

When we turned down the drink offer, she went inside to do the necessary preparations for our delivery, including lavishing her lips with ruby red lipstick. While she was thus engaged, we talked with her two servants, which seemed more of an appropriate word than maids, but without the servility of an unwanted, forced employment. They told us, "The Senora has us polishing, polishing every day." Indeed, the antique furniture emitted the satin glow of fine old patinas.

When the matron returned, she introduced us to a husband and wife team who would guide us through the delivery. They were Spanish, not Mexican- it seemed important to make distinctions anywhere near the San Luis Valley and farther south- who at first seemed not to fit together; she seemed 25 to 40 years old, while he seemed anywhere from 40-60 years of age. Her teeth were gently bucked with the two front ones crossed slightly. Her short bobbed hair and her glasses that made her eyes bug just a little, gave her a perpetually surprised look.

Her husband was a wonder. My first impression was that he was a relative of Goofy with his elongated head and ear lobes which seemed too large for his body-too tall really, because it sat upon a stocky, sturdy, slightly hunched body. He had an ancient Spanish look-the textbook Castillian, with a slender, noble look of pride. His expression was continuously serious, even while pulling the practical joke (very practical) that made us laugh for years afterwards.

When we had first entered the driveway of the hacienda, we saw the landscape that is the type to be the envy of most home-owners- a very fishable pond off of the deck of the house. This, then was our delivery spot, but in order to drive there, we had to negotiate extremely cautiously through a narrow wooden corral gate. We pulled our extensive side mirrors in on our heavy-duty two-ton Dodge truck, and Steve had to take a few tries at it to back up exactly straight into the corral. There was little room for error, since the gate posts were too tight and confining, but removing them would likely take time and machinery, a jack and digging bar, or even a tractor, using its hydraulics.

Because we had spilled quite a quantity of our supply of water while backing into the mud and manure-filled corral, we couldn't drive out. The hired man, our man Goofy, sent his wife to bring her Jeep Cherokee to tow us. She had been laughing and joking all during the delivery, and seemed like a happy kid. Her husband still maintained his serious look, but was very intelligent and knowledgeable.

When his wife arrived with the 4-wheel drive with which she delivered the mail in the area, her husband set a chain under our truck and attached it to the ball joint on the back of her Cherokee. As she turned her back to us to get into her Cherokee turned tow truck, her husband made another chain magically appear which he expertly wrapped around the troublesome post in the corral gateway. When he gave her the signal, she gunned her vehicle, slipping us out fast, spraying mud and manure everywhere. The chain jerked tautly on the post, ripping it out, sending it spinning and twirling in the air like a wooden bat released from home plate.

When the driver stopped and came back to look at the post with the chain still attached, she said with a slight Spanish accent and the surprised, child-like look that seemed always with her, "Deed I do that?"

Her husband gave the faintest hint of a smile.

Trout Delivery from Nebraska

Swear words whirled a country swing as the trucker from Valentine, NE, announced his arrival. Cussin' was part of the farm vernacular called "Trout Talk", the happy communication that guided and enhanced the delivery. The trucker was damn delighted to have arrived, and Steve was happy as hell to see him.

Valentine was one place where we raised fish to be trucked to Colorado for delivery. The truck was equipped with a two-part stainless steel tank, complete with oxygen set-ups hissing their arrival. Steve tossed the back-up blocks into perfect position and gave the trucker the middle finger signal which meant that he could back up onto the blocks for the perfect slanted angle.

How many ways can a PVC pipe be used? Most descriptions would neglect to mention their usefulness as a fish drain, but it's the gentlest way. Run 'em through with water to protect the fish with their slime coating and watch them glide into the water. When Steve waggled his other fingers, it meant to release the fish. When a valve was opened, fish and water shot out, rainbow colors twisting and glistening in the June sun. A few fighter trout could be heard battling their way up-pipe until a bucket of water washed the last of them down.

The first thing healthy trout do when gill meets water is to adjust their air sacs by surfacing and gulping air. People who don't know this attribute it to the fish being hungry and jumping for a new Mayfly hatch. When Ricky T, one of the farm employees, delivered fish to a horse tank at a sports and travel show in Denver, the fish were doing what they were expected to do: show off with movements of surfacing and gulping air. A small boy there cried, "Look Mommy, they're talking!"

Ricky's four-year-old son shot back, "No they're not; they're breathing!"

A "Cline Trout Farm Headquarters" sign from the '60's lies in the red barn taking a few hits of cat spray from time to time. Steve's father, a Colorado State University graduate in Forestry, as well as a Lt. Colonel in the Air Force, had chosen the wording of the sign that had been stationed in the driveway at the first trout farm on the corner of Folsom and Valmont, which is now the Unitarian Church and Trout Farm Apartments.

Delivering fish to places to which few people have access was one of the best privileges the farm life afforded. Many places were properties of extremely wealthy people: a movie star, financial moguls with conjoined properties, a former Miss America, a hotel and time share developer in Mexico, a golf course and ski resort designer, and a CEO of a large gas and oil company in Texas. There were dude ranches owned by individuals or large corporations. Second and third homes in Aspen, Vail, Cordillera, and Edwards, Colorado; and DuBois, Saratoga, and Jackson Hole, Wyoming, bespoke money and power, and the ability to impress friends and clients by spending it on a good time with the frivolity of trophy fish. Private, vastly expensive golf courses teased the common man even more by containing fishing ponds within their exclusive boundaries. We were told that when the stock market was doing well, a broker who had a ranch near Gunnison, would sometimes make a million dollars a day.

Steve would usually deal with caretakers rather than the owners. If they were single, we marveled at their freedom to enjoy a beautiful property which they hadn't bought. With dude ranches where husband and wife couples catered to the whims and wishes of the owners and their friends and clients, we later saw surprising divorces between the most amicable couples. Maybe they were too exhausted to continue catering to each other.

When trout deliveries took us into Las Vegas, New Mexico, we wound our way up the mountain, passing by a convent where a movie had been filmed on its beautiful acreage. As a young 25-year-old treated as a respected "Mizzus Cliii-ne" by well-mannered Texans, I glowed with the privilege.

Being respected and welcomed wasn't always the reception, however. On a beautiful, well-fished area of the Frying Pan River by Basalt, Colorado, we delivered to an enviable private property, where two fishermen in oozing wet hip-waders leaped into our truck almost the instant of our arrival, to join in on the delivery, and thought it was my place to stay behind to look after their dog. I didn't have a moment to protest or to find their truck for them, nor did Steve. When the truck drove away, they didn't grant me a backward glance, as if I should know my station as a trucker's wife. They even left me wet patches to sit on in the truck when they returned, and my duty with the dog was fulfilled. I did, however, like their dog; it was far better behaved than his owners. Steve was deeply apologetic to me.

Directly after fish are delivered, some new owners feel it is correct to help the fish breathe and swim. After fish have been in a tank for a few hours, they are tired. Some may even be seasick from a rough road. It should be obvious to some that once they enter water, they deserve a rest, but "Frank Fisherman" knows more than the fish and the people who raised them. While the trout were hanging out in shallow water, they might be shown lifesaving methods of water and air through the gills by the new owner, misguided and overly conscientious, to the detriment of the fish at rest. Some would hold the slimy fish with their non-slimy hands, thus removing the health protecting cover, and move the fish back and forth like a wind-up Match Box car, as he reminds the fish that it must breathe in, breathe out, because how else would it remember without the owner's physical reminder? I await the time that the fish's new owner shakes his own tail or rear end as a visual reminder to the fish how to swim again.

Some owners will poke and prod at a fish at rest. It is usually a gentle movement; after all, they have paid for the critters, but there is no telling a dedicated poker and prodder that it is better to allow the fish to rest until he's able to move into the main current to face whoever knows what dangers exist in the mainstream.

Some owners didn't want us to drive on their newly planted lawn. Why a stream needs Kentucky Bluegrass by its side is a secret known only to the owner and the consultant who has guided him. So Steve retained his physique and strength, running fish in a large dip net over and for the green. It was Steve's goal and pride to deliver live trout the kindest way he could.

Cleaning a Trout Pond (Raceway)

It's not easy to be on the farm on the days we clean the raceways.

A trout farm raceway can be ten feet wide and forty feet long. Its warped, ragged-edged sides look like a waterlogged dock's edge, with water lapping against them.

Frightened, fixed-eyed, staring trout race away from the six feet monster striding in rubber hip boots that pulls a multi-bristled broom toward himself.

As the hungry broom takes bites out of the water, the water swirls, forming miniature, clear whirlpools in front of the murky, particle-laden wall of water that the broom's action has dredged from the gravel bottom. A harsh, acrid smell arises from the mixture of wet fish feed and fish waste-an odor that seems to crawl under the skin-an odor one tries not to taste.

Fish tails whip and gills pump as the silvery rainbows first seek a safe hiding place in the darkness of the moving waste, and then dart toward crystal water. The swooshing suction sound becomes a rhythm as the rubber-legged giant continues the lifting, pulling action.

Fish blindly bump their noses against shins encased in hip waders. The sharp impact of slight pain is not unpleasant.

A hand trickling in the water can feel the slippery, stout bodies before one tail lash speeds them away. Darting around obstacles creates rolling ripples and plashes leading to one large exodus in a unified plunge of sound.

The pond is clean again with lines of water polishing each piece of gravel. The fish's mouths repeatedly open and close to a beat of, "Thank you for the exercise and clean-up."

Unloading Fish Feed

Before the days of our using fork lifts, unloading a semi-load of Moore-Clark or Silver Cup trout feed was a manual labor of love. The fifty pound bags required individual handling as we hugged them like smelly brothers. Two of us would climb into the back of the truck and hand/throw them out to the unsuspecting victim waiting below. Tossing a bag required strength, agility, and deceit to outwit some of the savvy, beefy or wiry hired hands. To accept a bag thrown at high velocity without a loss of wind or a back-step was an honorable thing. To carry two bags at once into the barn was a minor achievement. To tackle three was a study in dance while the carrier fought for balance as he turned and side-stepped over the upraised steps and door guide to deposit his load in the 3-way pattern that kept the bags connected while in the storeroom. That strong and heroic man deserved the first beer afterward.

A muscle-bound friend who was loaded with 8 bags, circled and wandered, misdirecting himself into the barn to flop the bags down in a pattern of disarray. Watching him made the rest of the guys dizzy, but with a desire to challenge him.

Our nephew, a chubby teenager who would grow up to become a 300 pound man, needed a workout when he came from a Northern state to help out at the farm. With his being barely able to squeeze into hip waders, Steve knew he needed an exercise trainer, whom he self-designated.

"Bring 'em!" would be the cry of bravado of the awaiting empty arms.

"It's coming!" would be the only warning given from inside the truck before valuable lessons in weight loss, strength and manhood were taught.

Our nephew received one of the varieties of throws that Steve could deliver, which flattened the poor kid to a spread-eagle, supine position onto the ground. We were never ones to make fun of people, so no one laughed……..at least for a minute fraction of a second, then we knocked the wind out of ourselves dying with hilarity. After grinding teeth and fighting tears, our nephew rear-ranged body parts after secretly appraising the damage, and rolled up to standing position, bag in hand, a triumphant feat, to the praise and cheers of the brown baggers' crew!

The feed was nicely stacked inside the barn, and we all felt more in shape with just "manhoods" challenged or jokingly belittled.

The Animals Try to Tame and Entertain Us

Snapper

Steve's and my camouflage canoe was bought for $35 from a San Lazaro Trailer Park resident who needed money fast since he had stolen band equipment from Hippie Bob and thought it best to move out of town. The two-person canoe created a balancing act with Steve trying my patience with constant shifting which he believed was for my own good so I would learn how to deal with rough water. I wished he would stop being so good to me.

Our pond was full of a variety of fish, including immense carp which could have fed a starving family of pioneers for a week. We were used to their brushing the canoe, being surprised by us and crashing through the shallow water to escape. We had more than a brush the day we had the privilege of being acknowledged in the water. Our fiberglass canoe may have been mistaken for an over-grown Big Bertha female when we were bumped by a turtle head. What surfaced has remained an astonishment to us. The white-scarred ancient head of an 80 pound snapping turtle emerged, complete with camo-colored shell. It paused in the water long enough to make eye contact- the gentlest, sagest, all-knowing look of an ancient being that had lived life long enough to have learned who enemies were, and who had passed us in a very privileged test. It calmly submerged again, leaving us with a feeling of having had a deep, all-accepting communication within the world of animals. We could have tamed a killer shark at that moment!

Fish Deliveries
Pelican Round-up

In the most severe drought year in Colorado before Hanholtz Reservoir #2 was drained and dried up, Steve delivered 3" trout in a cove formed by a long dock. With fishermen there "helping", we then all stood in helpless awe as white pelicans moved in. It's illegal to harm a pelican, and besides, the Fish and Game guys were there. With well-planned maneuvers, demonstrating their camaraderie, the 8 white birds seemed to hook wings and paddle in formation. We thought we saw their feet paddling in 4/4 time as they circled the newly planted fish for a delicious round of sushi.

Pelican Gorging

Cline Trout Farm's policy during Chief's (Steve's father) and Steve's days of running the business were always to deliver live fish. Fish that died within a day or so of delivery were guaranteed to be replaced. After nephew Jason delivered fish in a pond by a vacation home around Virginia Dale, the farm received a phone call stating that the owner couldn't find any fish in his pond, so we must not have delivered them. Steve, with his analytic mind, delivered the second round, determined to find the cause of the disappearing fish.

Since we required someone to be there the second time, the caretaker was there, with the owner planning to show up later. Steve delivered the fish and waited for the owner. What he and the caretaker saw was a phenomenon of superior hearing or sense of smell, because a dozen pelicans showed up and began to gorge themselves. The two watched in fascination as 12" trout, which took over a year to grow to that size, were scooped up into the pelican bills' reservoir, fighting and flapping, stretching and reforming the rubbery looking scoop, and then swallowed. When the owner arrived, the pelicans gladly continued their gluttonous demonstration. Steve told him he wouldn't have any fish left in a few hours.

Gill Pinching Crawfish

Steve had traveled over some Class 5 roads complete with mountainous boulders and cavernous ruts, but one journey was the worst. Fish can become disoriented, exhausted and even seasick in the transport tank. When Steve delivered the trout into the mountain pond, they lay where they were sent with no energy left to move. He and the caretaker/guide watched as crawfish skittered up to the helpless fish to hook onto their gills and tails. No human movement discouraged them. The exhausted trout were coated with crawfish cling-ons. After they had rested and were ready to move to deeper water, they seemed to gather their strength and give a mighty whip of their entire body, sending the crawdads home to daddy!

Finnegan

Ike, our part Chow dog, had always been a troublemaker from the time of her first visit home from the Humane Society. When she had something treed, a look would form on her face that was both elusive and intent, even a little ashamed if she were caught by me.

The day I saw her from the upper deck while I was looking at the apple trees, she wasn't looking up, but was lying down with that look upon her face. What I saw was a raccoon, no, a lynx......I had to grab binoculars. I focused in on the largest tiger-striped cat I'd ever seen. It became obvious that Ike was smart enough to avoid disturbing the cat; she wanted the tree to support the cat's weight, and not fall on her! When I walked outside, the cat ran home.

Days later I heard our neighbor calling it. A large man with little affect, he called Finnegan home.

"Finnegan, kitty, kitty, kitty." We had heard that his wife owned a restaurant. Finnegan had eaten well.

When I watered and weeded my tomatoes across from the apple trees where Finnegan liked to hide in the tall grass, he would sometimes emerge from the jungle to grant me the honor of a visit. These visits would consist of pets, tummy rubs and leg bends as he rubbed against them and my back injuries from lifting him.

A few days later while deadheading roses near the tomatoes, I heard a Magpie commotion. Our Magpies were the loudest, most vocal, while being the most articulate birds in our ornithologist's haven. A strong throaty voice accosted my ear:

"Ra, ra ,ra, ra, RAAT!"

A trilling, apologetic response followed: "Reh, reh, reh."

"Ra, ra, RARA, ra, ra, RAAT!"

The same tongue and throat rolling reply followed, complete with sincerity, "Reh, reh, reh."

When I went to our driveway, I saw the Magpie in our neighbor's drive. He was walking like a Sumo wrestler, wings tucked back, torso jutted forward like a wrestler's pose with deliberately protruded testicles. He had swaggered within 8 feet of Finnegan who was unthreateningly lying down.....all 40 pounds of him.

The conversation continued with more emphasis.

"RA, RA, RA, RA, RAAT!"

"Reh, reh, reh."

My human interpretation:

"Leave my kids alone, you feline bully!"

"Sorry. It really wasn't me."

"Are you listening? Leave Heklyette and Jeklyette alone!"

"I'll try, but hey, I'm a cat. It's kinda what we do."

"If I see you by their nest again, I'll have the whole MAG-PATROL on ya!"

"Maybe I can try a little harder. Really sorry."

Turquoise Lake

November, 2007
Our property on the south side of a county road in Valentine, NE, contains a series of spring branches that join together to form Turquoise Lake. In fact, it's totally the north facing spring branches that feed the Niobrara River. When I happened to mention my created name for the pond to the hired man who felt too proprietary, he said, "Oh, huh, I've always just called it My Lake."

I'm not sure what gives it its lovely turquoise color in warm weather; it seems to reflect sky blue and turn it into a Caribbean blue. It's just barely wide enough for a kayak or two, but not for traveling far since upstream is sand and silt that would catch the bottom and hold them.

Steve and I walked to the dike, then I began climbing while he kept his ragged knees on level ground. It wasn't long before deer trails began to guide me; it's difficult in many places to walk beside Turquoise Lake. The tracks led me above the pond while giving me a view. In some places above, the trees had no grass underneath as if rain had washed it down to a level of powdered bedrock. The first streams I came to looked refreshing with lush grass and a deer paradise of drinking water. Their hooves had formed pockets where mud had settled. As the streams paralleled each other, running from the south, I chose the middle path, until the source of the western stream, a spring, revealed itself.

The eastern part of the stream cut a walkable ravine which rose and dropped again back toward itself. Fallen paper birch trees, nearly extinct there, created a partial dam where water that slipped through, rippled and bubbled an invitation to eat my sandwich there. Farther on, on top of fallen oak trees across the water, was a boulder-sized rust and wine-colored rock of unknown origin; an unusual sight in the white chalky area. The spring revealed itself at the top of the ravine, and as I stepped into the open, the wind reminded me it was there and viable.

The top of the ravines where springs originate and flow toward ponds, is a wholly different environment. With a flat golden grassland top and endless scratchy cedars, the source of springs and streams is enigmatic. I trust the deer and coyotes to form my pathways. There have been sightings and evidence of mountain lion in the area around Valentine, and in the main family hayfield, Splash, the young gelding, slashed his brisket open on barbed wire in a panic from seeing a cougar. Since I feel no fear, only curiosity and delight in my surroundings, I hope I never have reason to doubt my trust of wildlife.

I decided to walk upstream in the main feeder for Turquoise. The man who assembled the metal "Possum Lodge", must have hiked the area a multitude of times, looking for arrowheads and interesting rocks. He had dragged a large amount back to the little house on the family property to clutter the lawn, but left a broken bucket with rocks spilling out of it slightly upstream from the southern waters. I had forgotten that the head gate was on the property we were selling our hired hand. It had been set in concrete decades ago, and looked like an aged Italian structure from the moss that had formed. On the hillside above were bedsprings, the remnants of the iron single bed where a Potter, a previous owner, must have slept when he was fishing and camping overnight.

As the sun was going down, I knew Steve would begin to wonder and worry; he couldn't gawk as long as I can in each interesting place. I headed down stream and started to walk the dike by Turquoise, but had to cut cross country to a copse of cedars when I heard the worst crow racket I had ever heard. Interspersed in the raucous cries was a subtly discernible different cry, more fearful and pleading. When I approached, the birds flew, but I followed them again, and when they flew this time a small owl was fleeing for its life and sanity. This continued through two more stands of trees before I could no longer follow.

"Bullies!" I cried, "Leave him alone!"

As we were leaving Valentine, trying to beat the December 2007 "heavy snow warning of 4" to 6", I heard the raucous, obnoxious cries of crows again. I yelled and whistled for them to stop, but the sound of their bullying continued. I heard no cry of another bird, but as Ike, our dog, and I walked toward the gate, I looked back and saw a bald eagle soaring overhead in ever tightening circles, then loosening the circle to relieve the tension, followed by a teasing tightening again, until the crows were all riled and stirred, flying away, relieving the poor owl, if it had survived.

Valentine, NE Exploring

Nearly everyone craves a secret location where the burdens of life can be shed and left behind while a peacemaking haven can take control. The gentle whispers of a stream meandering by, water laughing and crowding through a culvert, or the icy, leaping shout of a waterfall as it plunges fifteen feet to a sandstone bottom- this is the conversation I want to hear as I wander through our place in Nebraska.

After Steve and I cross Minnechaduza Creek and the Niobrara River, we travel into a wildlife refuge where bison glance at us calmly, then bob their shaggy, knotted heads to return to grazing, unafraid. Herds of elk don't bother to scatter, knowing that even their eight feet antler span might not bring hunters onto a refuge.

The narrow road grabs our tires and vibrates our jaws as we wind through the curves, grinding sand between our teeth as we jounce around on the washboard bumps.

When we arrive at our gate, there are antique wagon wheels on the fence, left there by the previous inhabitants. In the spring or in fall, the salad fresh smell of grass permeates the air, as cattle munch peacefully on the hill to the west. The trail travels by the stream, dropping down toward a meadow and the river below. In front of us we see the white, chalky cliffs of the Niobrara River decorated with trees, some dangling like Christmas ornaments ready to drop into the river with the next pounding rainstorm. We turn right and follow the stream to our campsite. We have to line up our tires just right in the dip which parallels the stream or we will scrape the bottom of our truck maybe ending up in the stream. Climbing a slight knoll, we balance our camper so that we're not leaning too far one way.

After a dusty ride, it's refreshing to drop into the creek and wash the sand off my face. I stand on the tire that has been shoved into the stream bed, reach into the stream to feel water flowing through my fingers, and, with cupped hands, I dip and splash the icy water to remove the road grit. Steve is content to relax at the site and not bathe all weekend if it suits him. I must explore.

To the left, and following the stream down, I can hear the pounding of water as it collects, narrows and throws itself over the ledge, fanning out in a twelve feet wide skirt. At the base of the falls are Birch trees, remaining where the last of the glaciers melted.

Following the stream farther down, I can look up and see a rusty metal grate used for a bridge to the "secret" walk-in campsite, shaped like a large teepee base. To the right of the stream there is a small meadow surrounded by trees where the turkeys I surprise gobble with high-pitched startles and fly away. Deer blow their reaction through their nostrils and leap away, being chased by our Chow/ German Shepherd, as she darts and rushes, ignoring my scolding, taking her task very seriously, as if she will deliver dinner tonight.

The stream wanders through a lower meadow where the sun feels hotter against my skin. I climb a fence and weave my way through brush, the brown, wide Niobrara in front of me, its white ripples rising from the surface. Near my footsteps are darkly gleaming droppings that we later found out were from a moose that had taken up residence there.

As I test the water of the river, it is lukewarm. The feel is not shocking, but calming. As I lie, face up to body surf, my hands are touching bottom, and I feel sand sifting and rasping my fingers as I glide along, exposing the sandstone base. After my surf is done, I walk back toward the campsite by another route, following a rocky, grass covered, tree-laden ravine, listening to birds chirping and twittering, then going silent as I hike toward their nests. I am more careful now, because a mountain lion has been sighted in the vicinity.

As I reach the campsite, I feel that Steve's and my hard work for these many years has been well worth it. We have the perfect spot, where, for now, the main worry is what to explore next. People don't need large parcels of property in order to feel that they are getting away from stress; they just need a spot in which their passion renews itself each time it is visited. I hope everyone can find that place.

Meeting With Federal Workers

When Steve and I met with workers from the Federal Forest Service to learn about entering the Forest Fuels Program to thin our forest of Eastern Red Cedar to save room for the hardwoods, Jen, a ranger, showed us the difference between a male and female tree. The females have blue berries, or early in their formation, soft bluish ends. The males, however, have stiffer cone-like formations!

Keeping your eyes peeled takes on
a whole new meaning
...after laser surgery.

True Tails

Should Animals, Factory, and Industry
be used in the same sentence?

Random Episodes

At the farm in Boulder we had a large family of barn cats. It seemed to be a privileged group; mainly a cat had to be born into it. On the asphalt driveway I observed most of the cat gang encircling a freshly dead snake. Their paws curled while making tentative batting motions, though a foot away from the harmless garter snake.

*****

When Mitten, my unwilling traveling cat knew she was close to the Nebraska property, she would become excited and stand beside the passenger window, then jump into the back, then return to the front. When I had an Android phone, I didn't have Siri, I had Google Assistant with a female voice. It was difficult and nearly impossible to find WiFi connection in the area. At one point I told Mitten, "Settle down. Ten more minutes and you can play, play, play."

My assistant helped me settle her with this helpful monotonal guide: "I found three places where you can play, play, play."

*****

There are times when I stop at the top of the driveway in Valentine to avoid frightening whatever bit of wildlife that may be there. In November I watched three elk with their fluff butts, then observed their unique lunging walk as they became aware of my presence.

I saw an eagle fly overhead as the elk moved away. What a welcome!

*****

The day I arrived extra early, I avoided slamming a truck door or performing extra movement. I was vastly rewarded as I moved silently down to the river at the fork. At the base of the sandstone rocks was a party of differently represented inhabitants. I saw one elk and a deer, never before seen together; two geese and three ducks. I wondered if they had been having these parties together during my absences.

Steve and I drove a few miles north of our place until we crossed the highway to enter South Dakota. There was much ranchland, some farmland and scattered homes. Steve stopped by a plowed field, and we observed a badger digging a hole. It used its pointed nose to dig and throw out dirt. It wasn't a honey badger, but looked tough and industrious nonetheless. It seemed to be unaware of our presence, but finally stopped to watch us momentarily without fear, then continued with its work ethic, uninterrupted.

*****

Ed and Lynette told us of the EID disease that had killed 60% of the deer in Nebraska, as well as some cows. It was so prevalent that the state planned to buy back hunting licenses. The disease was caused by gnat-like insects crawling into the deer's noses, which attracted them as one of the few places that retained moisture in the severe drought. We found 4 carcasses on the brief stretch of the river that we had named "Picnic Island".

*****

On one of Steve's and my hikes on our property, we suddenly heard an immense rumbling and thought that Ed was bringing in cows or horses in his trailer. When we walked toward the sound, we saw clouds of white dust wafting from across the river. A giant portion of the cliff had torn away, tumbled down and settled beside the river. As we observed in amazement, our boots became covered with the powdery residue from the cliff's avalanche.

As we hiked beside the river a month after the avalanche, we saw an eagle on the sandstone cliff, watching us without fear. He flew off his rock, seeming to show off for us as he soared, catching a jet stream above the water. As Steve peed in the brush, another eagle flew from the trees on the cliff and as they came together, they gracefully turned rolls, taking turns crossing over each other.

Big Red

Big Red was a steer, the type of mixed breed steer that produced a lean, lanky, hip bone jutting body that lifted, rolled and dislocated with each lengthy, meandering stride. He retained the curiosity of the species that hadn't been daunted or destroyed by cruel mistreatment or egotistical handling by his owners. His lack of fear of humans could have been frightening to any person who feared cattle and even a little unsettling to those who know animals enough to know that cows run at an arm movement unless giving birth or protecting their calf while nursing. Big Red, however, knew no fear, and also refused to nurse a calf!

Red's relentless approach to investigate anything that whetted his curiosity was a joy to see, if you could follow him around. One such day we did have the time. It was the first week of July, and the weather did everything it could to avoid doing anything original at that time of month; it was sweltering as always, and so were we. Hay season was upon us. We loved that work that allowed us to flex our muscles, see how far we could throw a bale onto the skidder, then stack them in our barn loft. It felt fulfilling to have a year's supply of feed for Big Red, or whichever cow or calf we would obtain. Our hay work was physical, but social. I made lunch for the small crew and we sat on the slight rise below the fence south of the Boulder airport, gobbling sandwiches and guzzling beer. We hadn't noticed how much we were being watched until Red lumbered over toward us, his curious nose raised with his tongue twisting and twirling, waiting for a taste of anything we had to offer. Lumpy, a friend, never one to pass on an entertainment opportunity, reached into his pocket and pulled out the can that had formed a faded circle on his Levi's brand. Holding his Skoal can, he twisted off the top. His fingers reached inside to pull out the slightest pinch. When he reached it toward Red, Red's neck and nose stretched forward and his strong neck seemed to remind Lumpy where that pinch should end up. Red's tongue reached out to accept it, but instead, Lumpy placed it on his nose. His tongue swirled and twisted as if he were anticipating the aroma and enhanced flavors that would enter his nostrils. When Red had it in his mouth, his jaws began to grind and rotate, chewing his cud, not to miss a snippet of flavor.

Red seemed like a fun-loving, harmless prankster. We hoped his pranks wouldn't turn on him and be his demise. We were fortunate enough to have a hay field that attracted geese. During hunting season it was amazing how many human friends we acquired! On the day that Steve's brother was hunting, he hid inside the feed shed, a 9′ x 5′building. Inside were stacked sacks of various sizes of fish feed pellets. To the east side was a hole, just fitting for the barrel of a shotgun. When Steve's brother felt the time was prime, he stuck the barrel outside the hole to sight in on one of the multiple geese the hayfield had attracted. His view, down his sight, however, was blocked and he had to retract the gun, then resight it. When the blockage on his sight-in didn't diminish or disappear, he stepped outside the shed to see what was happening. Outside, on the east side of the shed, was a large red steer with big eyes and a bony head full of curiosity.

When it was time to make a final decision regarding Red, it turned out to be one of the most painful decisions we would make. Farmers and ranchers have to be emotionally tough if they want to avoid attachments and make a little money on their livestock. Steve and I had one of the deepest conversations we would have. I asked him…..I begged him, if we could not take him to be butchered. Meat wasn't all that expensive and we could always buy meat through our friends from a steer we didn't know. He gently explained to me that the reason we bought Red was to fatten him up, and use the meat from his gain. We didn't buy him for a pet, and we had to be practical and stick with our plan for him. I tearfully agreed, but when it came time to take Red to the butcher, I couldn't go. When it came time to pick up the packaged meat, I wouldn't go. When it was time to stack the meat in the freezer, I avoided that too.

I managed to cook one or two of the steaks for Steve, but I could only glance at it, then look away. The pain and guilt I felt was really physical, and I lost some weight during the time I tried to become vegetarian. My farm raising, along with my own pep talks finally let the guilt assuage a little until I could eat meat again, specifically, Big Red.

Buddy Blue Jay

After living in our home in Boulder for twenty-seven years, we had the privilege of being visited by a flirty blue jay.

In the spring I was walking down by our pond, in the area where we had fill dirt, when I stopped three feet from the young jay. He didn't fly away, but looked at me and continued pecking away at roly-poly bugs. As I continued my walk looking at rocks, he flew within two feet of me. When I spoke to him, he cocked his head and looked at me with one eye, then pecked meaningfully on a rock.

The next day I was clearing the deck, getting it ready for staining. This included moving some tiles I was going to use for mosaics. When I heard a noise behind me, I laughed at the jay that was perched upon the tile container. When he was sure he had my attention, he pulled a 1 ½"tile out of the container and dropped it on the concrete. My laugh must have encouraged him because he pulled another tile out, but dropped it back into the container. He found other tiles to peck at in a show-offish, demanding attention style. When he flew away, I applied myself to applying Thompson's Water Seal.

At noon, Steve and I were eating in the Colorado room when there was a fluttering at our window. It seemed he was looking in at us, and could actually see us. He began pecking at the window. I moved slowly toward him. He didn't flinch, but instead looked me in the eyes. When I unlatched the window, the noise frightened him, and he flew away.

The next day was busy and it wasn't until afternoon that I was walking past the pea garden when he alighted upon the post that was holding the netting. When I spoke to him, he tilted his head, and then dive bombed past me, directly near my face! When he alighted sideways on a grapevine hanging down and coyly pecked at a dried grape leaf, I knew he was proud of his prowess, both at flight and flirtation. As I laughed again, he dived toward me directly above my head, making me close my eyes and duck.

Steve said the next morning he was gently pecking at my pink Crocs that I keep outside the back door. That same morning he had flown into Steve's shop. As Steve busily pieced metal together, he felt he had an insect on his arm and shook it off, but he was unknowingly shaking off our jay who flew out.

The next day must have been a busy one for our Buddy Blue Jay. I was looking east over the old feed bunks, down into the fill dirt hole when he appeared again, very briefly. Each day the blue of his feathers deepened in hue and vibrancy. He gave me the briefest moment of time on top of a steel-roofed outbuilding, cocking his head, absorbing my voice with utmost concentration and expediency, then flew away.

June 1st.—Another day on the deck with my tiles. He had just flown in to perch on the veranda railing and fluttered his wings superfluously when I had a phone call. While speaking, I had forgotten about the jay, and after I hung up there was a pause, and then the noise of his pecking at some tiles at the base of a pot seemed to be his reminder to me of his existence. He seemed to enjoy the sound of my voice when I apologized for forgetting him, and he stayed for a while, a few feet away. When he flew into the walnut tree, I knew I had had my visit for the day.

We left on Saturday morning, June 5th, to attend my best friend's daughter's wedding at a guest ranch in Sheridan, Wyoming. We stayed an additional night and didn't return until Monday. As we parked our car in the driveway and began unpacking, Buddy landed above the windshield and began talking quietly. It seemed like a heartbroken, gentle scolding, and I found myself explaining where we had been and why we had been gone. Later that evening he was attracting my attention on top of a pole and maybe claiming his superiority to the other jays while loudly and raucously cawing, the way a good jay should.

On a rainy day I was doing inside things, but felt the need to see Buddy after the rain slowed. I walked the whole perimeter of the part of the farm where I had seen him and had nearly given up when I walked past the north trees, and saw him perched on the open window sill of the motorcycle shed, as if he'd been waiting for me the whole time. He showed off a bit there, then hop-danced on the metal roof and onto an electric line, for which I scolded him. He didn't care or seem to notice me.

Another morning Steve and I were late going outside. The back door was open with the screen door shut. As Steve was about to leave the house, Buddy stuck his beak into the screen. When I stepped outside, he was no longer there, but he had landed on my bicycle pack and then my handle bar where I took a picture as he seemed to pose proudly. Later that day I saw him in the blue spruce outside the Colorado Room where we eat. I still had a salad to finish and I carried it outside. I spoke to him a while as he perched on a branch, then he dive bombed my salad to try to land on the rim of the bowl. When I jumped and moved it, he stopped his diving.

The day I was carrying out sweet potato peelings to throw into the mulch, he landed on our flagstone table. I placed the container of the peelings in front of him and he proceeded to pick them out and drop them onto the table until the container was surrounded by orange. It didn't seem to be his type of food; he's more of a carnivore, so I told him he had made a mess, picked them up and continued to the mulch container. Maybe I had insulted him, since I didn't see him the rest of the day.

The next two days dumped nearly continuous rain, and the cats hung close to the barn. At one point I saw Splish, the mighty hunter, stalking something. I hoped that Buddy's tameness didn't allow him to drop his guard around another of my buddies, but one of his worst enemies. I didn't see the result of the stalking, and then we left for Nebraska for a week, so I was very concerned I wouldn't see Buddy again. During our stay in Nebraska, I dreamed he was on my shoulder, and our conversations with each other continued.

When we returned from Nebraska, Buddy landed on top of our car within moments of our arrival, chattering away, scolding us for leaving him. The next day he showed off on the aluminum arbor a neighbor had given us. Buddy loved to pick at cobwebs on the arbor, looking for bugs or just cleaning it up, then he would clean his beak. I found a stink bug and gave it to him. He ate it in two pecks, then cleaned his beak again.

When I hung out laundry, he would land on the clothes and clothesline, pecking at the clothespins. I was talking to a friend on the phone and let him talk so that she could hear his brilliance! I then gave him a ride to the house on my laundry basket.

We heard that Buddy would visit a neighbor, an unusual man who rarely bathed, kept a motorcycle in his mobile home, and smoked a lot of weed. But Buddy seemed to sense kindness in the man, and would even perch on his hand when he held it out.

At a time when we returned from a bike ride, he excitedly chattered in the ash tree above the empty dog kennel. But when I fed the cats in the driveway, he left me along for the rest of the day.

We saw Buddy less and less as summer approached fall. I saw him one day in a tree toward the pond, but he barely acknowledged me. The last time I saw him, he was with what seemed to be his mate. They appeared to be building a nest together, maybe about to stock it with diapers, and though he had no fear of me, he ignored me in his work endeavors. I was hurt and a little jealous of that attention placed elsewhere, but I had to say Good-bye to my wild friend, and relish the fond and entertaining privilege we were allotted for a short time.

Buffalo Tears

As told to Steve and me by a guide at a hunting ranch in Valentine, NE

"I had to climb a tree again. I knew the bull buffalo was stalking me again, but I smelled him in time. He could turn over the Suburban if he wanted to......but he really hates Billy."

"Why does he hate Billy?"

"Billy guided the hunt that killed his buddy. There were originally two larger buffalo that had been together from calves until they were thirteen years old. Billy guided the first hunt of the two bigger buffalos where he pushed the bulls toward the hunters. One of the hunters shot and killed one. When one big bull was down, the other bull stood by him. They couldn't get him to leave the dead one so that they could take the carcass out. Finally, Billy had to run the bull off with a tractor and put him behind a fence. The big bull raised his head and cried with each breath. From then on, he hunted Billy."

"I had always heard that when a buffalo is down, the rest of the herd beats him up. But that's not true. This is what I saw when a hunter shot a younger bull:"

"The hunter took a shot which was a lung shot, and the buffalo went down. The rest of the herd surrounded him and started nudging him with their heads. They kept doing this until he got up. The whole herd went back to grazing, surrounding the bull so that we couldn't tell which one it was. Finally, with our binoculars, we noticed a spot of blood from the lung area of the bull. The hunter took another shot and killed it."

"The herd nudged the kill again and again, but realized it was dead. The head bull sniffed the younger dead bull, raised his head, and over and over gave out high-pitched, keening wails."

"I really gained a lot of respect for buffalo that day. I don't think that I could kill one."

Ike, the Humane Society Alpha Female

No cautious, intelligent rancher would have adopted Ike. When we were delivering fish in Laramie, Wyoming, an immense ranching area, the customer told us that a woman had advertised 6 Chow puppies for sale and couldn't sell even one! Ike, our beautiful Chow, that female Humane Society adoptee, that cat killer, sheep harasser, trailer court wanderer, goose fetcher, that human feces roller, ended up with us!

After Jessie, our dog prior to Ike was hit and killed by a car on Valmont while panicked by fireworks noises, I decided to have a little interim to think about what kind of a Boulder Pet Guardian I really was. I thought I could do without a dog, and really, I was amazed that I held out for a few months. It wasn't so much that I was lonely without a dog, but incomplete, as if part of a communication skill was lacking.

In late summer both the Longmont shelter and the Boulder one were seriously limited in adoptable dogs that met my criteria: no young puppies (no time to house break them with school starting again) no older dogs (they had to run with me, Sacagawea) no hyper dogs or ones who needed constant petting and attention. My choices were narrowed down to feeling sorry for a strange looking, hyperactive, separation anxiety-ridden jumper and pleading eye muttster… or Ike. I thought the other dog would continue to have separation anxiety since I was returning to work, and Steve continued his fish deliveries to be gone at times for twenty hours or into the next day. So, Ike, the Chow/German Shepherd mix, the most beautiful dog in the Humane Society, and really, a potential beauty queen/movie star, was my choice.

Many people report that it was the eye contact or the excitement of the dog at first seeing them that caused them to choose their dog or the dog to choose them. Ike's case was entirely different. She never made eye contact, being much too coy, or thinking that I was her jailer and that I owed it to her to spring her from her enclosure.

Her mother was in the same kennel. I felt very guilty about taking one and not the other, but I rationalized it by thinking that everyone needs to leave their mother some day; it's only the 25-going-on-40 humans that overstay their welcome, living with their mommies!

That the Humane Society had their rules about walking dogs only in their area or for checking out a dog for a very limited time for a home visit, and a spay job before adoption, were irritating, but the rules became perfectly clear when I took Ike home for a test run.

First, I was only allowed to walk her at the Humane Society with a leash. When I placed the loaner nylon leash around Ike's neck, she refused to act grateful, or even acknowledge me. As we walked outside the building, we stepped onto a patio type area where an orange-suited jail inmate was standing after possibly having hosed the area down. Ike tried to choke herself to death on the leash, trying to move as far away from him as she could. She seemed to have had some issues with him or known something.

I thought, "Now here's a dog with a good judge of character!"

However, then I remembered that she still hadn't made eye contact with me. At least she wasn't choking herself to move away from me....horizontally anyway.

As she dragged me on our first walk in the back "yard" I could feel an all pervasive sense of her untamable wildness and power. I thought I should read all of Jack London's books again, especially The Call of the Wild, just to prepare for her.

When I checked her out at the desk like a library book that no one had requested for a while, I felt a sense of adventure and that a bonding and purely psychic communication were about to take place. They told me to be sure not to let her wander for fear of her becoming pregnant. I gave them the "Don't be an idiot and don't take me for one" look.

When we were in my yard I walked her around on the leash for a while and I could tell that she thought that I could never control her if I was going to bore her to death, so I removed the leash to give her an adventure under my watchful eye. I have never known a dog as elusive and stealthy as Ike. It took only a moment before her nose was on the ground and she was out of the driveway gates, looking for a male so that she could break the Society's rules and become great with puppies. How much respect can a wild thing give to a prospective owner who is running around, chasing and reaching for anything on the dog to hold onto- her ruff, her flank, her tightly curled tail (which would later prettily hold empty beer cans)? Once I got hold of her and leashed her, I rethought my need for a dog.

It was another week before she could be scheduled to be spayed. Though I'm strongly in agreement for spaying most animals and a few humans, it seemed a shame to not reproduce that cute face and Alpha personality.

When I picked her up from the spay clinic, I placed her in the hatch-back of my Chrysler Laser. She had always been modest regarding her bathroom habits, but from almost the instant she was in the back, she circled a few times, then defecated before I could pull over.

When I first brought her into the house, she wanted to check out the back bedroom. When I caught up to her, I found her on the bed, mischievously smiling and wagging her curly tail at me. It was the first eye contact she had made with me, and it was hard to scold her. I sounded her name, three syllable/tone style, and she jumped off the bed and ran to the living room. There I found her on the leather couch with the same smiling face and tail. It took only these two times of scolding to teach her to stay off the upper levels which were reserved for the lower beings such as humans. When I checked her non-jumpable stitches, they seemed to have resisted ripping.

Her stitches were meant to stay dry, and she was to remain calm and not run. Since I was about to begin the fall back to school routine, we had to have our vacation. We decided on Tin Cup and Taylor Reservoir where we had a friend whose family had cabins. We drove over Cottonwood Pass and dropped into the little peaceful town of Tin Cup. Ike didn't know who to follow, as many children ran around the area, and the first thing she did on the dirt street was to leap joyfully into the ditch that ran through town, soaking her wound with non-sterilized, unfiltered, non Avion or Perrier water. Again, though she had been with us for a couple of weeks, she chose not to recognize our voices. It didn't matter that we hadn't changed her name from the gender inappropriate "Ike"; she refused to come, no matter what we called her. When we climbed a thirteener, she stayed with us, but when we reached the bottom to walk to the vehicles, she followed whomever was in front but then refused to get into their car. She refused to get into any car, even though our begging, pleading voices should have by then become vaguely familiar to her as the ones who fed her and gave her Boulder Pet Guardianship. Though she was scrawny with dry, coarse hair when we first adopted her, she ate very little dog food because she was well fed with her own hunting of mice, voles, squirrels and probably Preble's Jumping Mice, just to defy the City of Boulder.

After our visit we were returning over Cottonwood Pass and stopped for the amazing view and to stretch. We didn't seem to be able to become used to placing a dog on a leash, and because we were lax, we paid a painful price. When she finally returned to us, she seemed smeared with what seemed like peanut butter, only more orange. There were no cattle on the pass, and we may have been able to forgive her for rolling in cow dung, or even deer or elk scat since she was a wild thing, but when the smell of human feces struck us, I was ready to check her back into the Humane Society. We popped up the camper, boiled water, put on rubber gloves, found some scissors and checked our gag reflexes. Cutting off the most offensive areas, we were still left with a bit of residue, and we both hoped Palmolive dish soap was truly antibacterial.

After we came back from our "vacation", I started back to my teaching job. Steve had firm beliefs that dogs shouldn't be on a chain, after our first two seemed to be on them more times than not. Since Ike wasn't sure who we were and what the guidelines were even if she allowed us to try to control her, she wandered around the farm and beyond. She liked to sneak into the trailer court behind us to see what dog could come out to play or just to tease them that she wasn't fenced, but they were. When we went to look for her, she would come home with her tail uncurled and slightly tucked, looking abashed and deeply sorry. That guilt would last until we weren't looking or until we took a breath and relented a bit from our scolding, then she would smile, wag her tail and nip us, sometimes in the butt.

Any farm with a barn is certain to gain cats, and we were well-known in the cat world neighborhood as shelter and for being gullible enough to feed them. One particularly beautiful, long-haired feral cat was trying to tame me, and just when she had allowed me to pet her, she met her doom by Ike the next day. No amount of scolding or placing Ike in her kennel seemed to curb the desire to grab moving, live objects. I had meant to call the Boulder Humane Society to tell them that their method of seeing if a Chow was truly a cat killer was a little skewed. The day I was about to adopt Ike, the volunteer held a kitten toward Ike's nose. When Ike was far too preoccupied to notice the kitten, the blue-vested helper decided that Ike was no harasser or killer. As life with Ike continued, she certainly wasn't limited to only cats.

When we had sheep on the farm, Ike liked to pay them visits. The sheep didn't wish to be visited by Ike who was a bully and a chewer. The shepherd instinct to herd seemed natural, but when there were dual personalities inside battling for the kill… (Thanks for herding them, now, move over,) it created a Hyde personality that was quite destructive. However, what Steve saw during the year that Boulder Creek was as high as we had ever seen it, made us think that there was some amazing shepherd breed inside her. We had unloaded a small truckload of sheep, including lambs. I don't know what we didn't understand about our killer dog, but for some neglectful reason we had forgotten about her and she was there awaiting all her prizes. Before we were ready to react, Ike had chased a lamb into the water. The water was so dangerously powerful that Steve knew the lamb would drown, but before his disbelieving eyes, Ike jumped into the water after it. She held the lamb's head out of the water! Steve ran the thirty yards to the bridge and lifted the lamb out, barely catching it before the rapid waters enveloped it, it while Ike crawled out farther downstream, looking bedraggled and as if she might consider behaving for a few days.

When Ike was still young, about ten months old, Mr. Tubbs, our friends' Chesapeake Bay retriever, took a liking to her. At a gathering Tubbs decided to hump Ike to an audience. Ike was so light that she kept falling down as Tubbs' forelegs wrapped tightly around her. This continued all across the lawn with my being the good owner chasing them both, and looking like a fool. Added to Ike's helpless falling to the ground appeared Tags, another of the farm's dogs, to chew on her face. Ike was nearly helpless until the other two owners woke up and pulled the dogs off. Ike tore into Tags and her powerful white teeth ripped her below her neck. There were no more power plays to fear from Tags.

One could hardly guess what Ike would bring to the house every few days. Usually the mice she caught were eaten immediately as if the mouse pate would spoil. We had been shown raccoons and squir-rels, but her biggest surprise, proudly carried with her head held high to keep the feet from dragging, was a young goose.

When we were in the mountains, we let Ike run beside the truck. The moment we let her out to follow behind or beside, she ran ahead of the truck. That emphasized the difference between fast and quick, when, after a blink, she was in front, chasing a chipmunk.

Ike liked to herd sheep, then chew on one, to their terror. I realized why no rancher would have a Chow. She was so difficult to control around them that I tied her closely to a pole in the sheep barn, causing hers and the sheep's uneasiness. It seemed to make her, temporarily, leave them alone.

A Wyoming veterinarian, specializing in knees, was so impressed with Ike's ability to hold empty beer cans in her tail, that he added a picture of her to his annual calendar.

A daily walk for me consisted of moving quickly around the ponds. I usually walked the same route, counter-clockwise, in the afternoons. On one of the days Steve and I walked together, dusk was approaching, and we walked clockwise. When we were near a smaller pond, a coyote rushed toward us, brushing up against Ike and running away. Ike sprinted after it, though we repeatedly called her back, fearing a lure. She ignored our frantic calls, and it had become so dark that we couldn't see her, nor the pond. Finally, five minutes later, she came to us, out of breath, wet, with blood under her chin….blood that wasn't hers. We figured out that a small coyote pack had lured her, trying to push her into the pond, and when she was helpless, attacked. She managed to escape, and thereafter, when she heard coyotes howl near us, her tail dropped, and she would slink toward the house.

When Ike was eight, her tail began to lose its curl. Our veterinarian was concerned that there might be spinal issues accompanying that. When we took her on our vacation back East, we weren't fully aware of her deteriorating back and leg problem. When we did a three mile hike, a previously no effort one for Ike, we stayed on top of a hill on the trail. At one point, Ike was at the bottom of the hill in a small surround.

"What's she doing down there?" I asked Steve with exasperation. "Did she find something to hunt?'

As we waited for her, she caught up and we walked back to the truck. She sat down as if from the large effort or from pain. She had to ride back hundreds of miles to Colorado in the back seat, and avoided jumping into vehicles from that time, but it seemed her stationary position made her back stiffen.

When we were next driving to Nebraska, we put her into our car, and she began to panic, pacing from window to window, panting from the fear of the pain she must have felt would come. We needed to go to our property there, and couldn't call off our trip, so we asked if my sister Terry and her husband Paul could dog-sit her. They thankfully agreed. One of their dogs began chewing on Ike, not to harm her, but attracted by a fungus that Ike had acquired, unbeknownst to us. No wonder she began to like baths, and willingly climb into the bathtub.

Paul called us to inform us what the vet had told him. We decided with such a sense of loss, that it was best to euthanize her.

Ike was our princess, the prettiest dog we had ever had, but by far, the most difficult.

Dear Kathleen,

Since we are always comparing and analyzing dreams like Sigmund Freud, I must tell you about one of the strangest and certainly one of the strongest real dreams I've ever had, which, in thinking about it, has brought back such vivid memories.

The dream was about Nurdly Smutbinder, you remember, our little dog that was supposed to be the size of a Labrador Retriever, but ended up, fully grown, the size of a Rat Terrier.

We selected him from the Humane Society in Boulder, or rather, he selected us by his obnoxious barking which reminded people of the insistent noise of a lawn mower early Sunday morning. He was only six inches tall and was in an upright puppy cage that was close to our faces (and ears). Due to the size of his paws that seemed to resemble a baseball mitt, he was supposed to be large. It was just like Nurdly to be too stubborn to grow.

I think the reason Nurdly was our favorite dog for those twelve years and to this day was because he matched Steve's personality so well. They were both tenacious brats, and both seemed to bite the hands that fed them, except mine.

He went everywhere with us; we even took him on our honeymoon. We wanted to take him into the hotel, but no dogs were allowed, and when Steve tried to stuff him into his duffel bag to sneak him past the hotel desk, Nurdly's legs splayed out like a stubborn mule's refusing to travel a steep mountain path. When Steve tried to put the duffel bag over the Nurd, he leaped away with surprising strength and agility-he must have had claustrophobia.

When Nurdly was twelve, he lost his hearing, which made it tough to call him back when he left home to find a girlfriend.

His hearing loss proved to be fatal to him. We were at our mountain property above Jamestown and had let the dogs run. Nurdly was on the trail of some wild animal with his tail waving back and forth as rhythmically as a car antennae in the wind.

He didn't hear the 4-wheel drive coming. We didn't see him because of the thick brush, and the wheel relentlessly crushed his spine, causing Nurdly to let out a scream of pain. We were all in shock, looking at the lifeless body lying on the ground, when, with a pathetic struggle of forelegs pawing the ground, he tried to pull himself up to continue the chase! A horrifying sight followed. Having his spine crushed meant that the spinal cord containing the nerves to his rear legs had been severed, and he could only crawl to his front legs and drag his rear legs behind.

The decision we made at the veterinarian's was rather quick: euthanize him rather than force him to drag himself everywhere, to forego his desire to hunt and play naturally.

After that we had the process of grieving that parents would go through who have lost a child-the morning and evening depression, and the expectations at the normal times of seeing Nurdly, and the awareness that he wasn't here.

Those were the memories; this was the dream. I was napping one afternoon when I heard a noise while I was halfway between consciousness and sleep. The noise was a familiar one-the click of a dog's toenails on the oak floor. I even felt a soft bump against the bed as it seemed Nurdly was jumping up to lie at the foot of the bed as he often did. It seemed that he lay there for minutes before I became fully conscious, with the silence seeming so thick and potent, as if a thousand locusts had just become still and quiet in anticipation of an ominous storm, yet that silence seemed to be filled with communication between my "ghost dog" and me, and it seemed that somehow I felt a comfort that was as much a release of emotions as a half hour of sobbing would have been.

After that dream, somehow his death and our resultant loss seemed a little easier to live with.

So, Kathleen, my dream was bizarre in its own way-not the jumble of people and events of the week that seem to mix together to form some sort of meaning that we analyze, but a message that was clear and comforting to me, a message that said in precise doggy language- "Git over it and git on with it!"

Sincerely,

Peggy

Molly

Molly was a typical name for a dog when we met her. But there was nothing typical about her. She was friendly, but tough and protective. She was loyal, but could show her strength and disdain while avoiding being contained in a fence or dog house, dog god forbid! Strong-willed, she was her own man, her own dog! A short-haired Lab mix, she was white rather than golden, and how she remained white with her active life was a wonder.

When we first met Molly, we were in our soon to be driveway talking to a realtor when, as a pup, she ran across the paved road to say Hi and jump on us. We were amazed and asked how she could have possibly crossed that busy road and lived. We neighbors were to find out she crossed it multiple times a day for over twelve years!

The first winter in our new place, our pond froze. Molly came to visit and get a drink on a particularly cold day. To my horror, she crashed through the ice. I stood on the bank, frantically calling her from the shortest, most direct angle from her as she floundered, breaking ice, swimming as she was able…directly away from me. When she reached the opposite bank, I chased her with a towel which I had to use to hold her as I tried to dry her. In terror, she escaped from me and ran back to her farm. I didn't see her for two weeks, learning that she could not only lay blame, but also hold a grudge!

Who wouldn't grow up big and strong with a daily breakfast of two raw hot dogs and two Fat Boy ice cream sandwiches? Molly gulped all her food, with the exception of dry dogfood which bored her, but which most of the 'hood had for her as she made her daily visitations of up to sixty people. Her rounds began early, whether anyone was up or not (some arising at ungodly hours before 7!) She was an all-weather dog, her strong stride keeping her warm, allowing her to ignore the rain or snow which at times coated her, yet didn't deter her purpose. There was not a person in the 'hood and beyond who didn't know who Molly was.

Her favorite place to go when she still liked the dogs they owned, was to Jimmy and Dee's at the end of the block, where their shop had the perfect winter setting: a wood stove for feeling cozy as well as for cooking. The couch could accommodate two dogs, and oh yeah, Jimmy. After the three of them were settled in, Molly would show up to be cozy and to demonstrate her amazing strength. The couch felt so accommodating to her that she would cuddle and wriggle in, tucking and stretching her powerful legs and hips, while finding the right spot. One dog was gently forced off the couch to the rug-covered floor. With one dog gone, it was so much easier to maneuver, so the other dog had to slither to the floor which was softened with carpet remnants. With two sleep mates eliminated, there was only one left to make room for her: Jimmy. Molly twisted, turned and flopped, but Jimmy held his ground, and wasn't forced to the ground.

Molly visited me second most. One reason was that I was on a slight hill where she could see her farm, and secondly, because I had rocks in my yard. We had driveways smothered with gravel, and I had oddly shaped rocks that just seemed to appear. We never knew why she would choose one rock over another but she always chose one that forced her to stretch her jaws in order to hold it. To most dogs or kids, it would have been a choking hazard, but it was her catalyst to play. She proudly danced with the rock, spinning, her feet and legs in the air, showing off, almost daring us to chase her, then pounded the ground while choosing a burial spot for her prize. I never saw her return to the spot to retrieve it; maybe we just had such an assortment that she wanted to try as many as possible.

On an unusually wintery Sunday that had produced snow that layered the ground, I broke out my cross country skis. As soon as I reached my little hills, Molly joined. She followed me as I tried to create some sort of rhythm of stride and glide, but sometimes she would stand on my skis, forcing me to a stop. The entire 'hood, as well as drivers on the road, seemed to be sleeping in that day, and it was ethereally peaceful. I couldn't be irritated at Molly for stopping me in mid-glide, so I decided to do what she did. I watched her farm across the road as she watched. I tried to listen hard to match her hearing prowess, and the first thing I heard was a barn cat mewing softly, which seemed muffled from the distance. Molly sniffed the air, so I took deep breaths, trying to appreciate the purity of the air that came with the freezing temperature. I listened to the sound of my skis breaking the short trail in our yard, and gained a new appreciation for Molly, who must have known her hips were deteriorating, but determined to continue her lifestyle as the inquisitive, loyal, active neighborhood mascot and farm dog.

Strong-willed, overly-protective, jealous! To make it more difficult Molly, the neighborhood and farm dog, obeyed few commands. She occasionally paid attention to, "No!" unless she was too busy performing the act that brought about the scolding. No dog could come near me without endangering itself with Molly's powerful jaws that glared so fiercely through her white, cavity-free teeth, and shone so brightly when her lips were laid back. The first time I fed her a treat, it was with trepidation, as she laid back her gums from her teeth, looking threatening. Her taking the treat from my hand was very careful and deliberate; it seemed she wanted me to note how careful she was being. One command that surprisingly she obeyed was, "Go Home!" She would turn tail, and dutifully head north to the farm, never looking back or questioning it when we were so exasperated with other wasted commands.

When my best friend, Margo, was here she brought her Schnauzer, Lucky, along. Margo had rescued Lucky from a hapless life where his owner was rarely home in her small apartment. Molly bullied Lucky who had no idea how to fight back as he cowered and whined. Margo finally had to use the, "Go Home!" command. I knew Lucky could have ended up torn and bleeding on the ground if the incident continued, but I still felt terrible watching Molly's deliberate canter back to the farm; she had slept on my doorstep the night Steve died.

If I had to deliver or pick up something from a neighbor in one of the 2.5-7 acre properties, I would walk. Molly would always find me and follow or lead the way since checking out the neighbors was her self-appointed daily duty. When I was at one neighbors' narrow drive, their Chiweenie came after me, hungry for ankles. I yelled and chased it back. As I turned my back, it fiercely tried to attack again. I thought I would never arrive at my neighbor's without bloody shoes. Tired of the time consuming game, I shouted, "Go Home!" to the obnoxious dog. Molly obediently spun around and trotted purpose-fully back to the farm.

"Not you, Molly!" I cajoled, but she never looked back.

The entire 'hood was terrified that Molly would be hit by a car or truck, since she crossed the road numerous times during the day. I decided to watch her to see how she had become so expert at her skill. Her expertise was no better practiced than on the large trucks that hogged our road. She didn't bother to look down the road, but used her finely honed sense of hearing to time their speed and arrival beside her. She turned her head slightly, the better to hear, and even had the appearance of boredom if they were surprisingly driving the speed limit. Her crossing the road lead to many people stopping, knocking on our doors, with questions of, "Is that your dog?" Molly's ownership questions were too complicated to explain, so my reply became, "No, she's the neighbor's. He's not home right now."

It's interesting to observe a dog so unfettered by conventional standards, both physically and verbally, by an owner who didn't need to have an ego fulfilled by domineering a dog he had acquired by default when his Uncle Paul passed away. Maybe as a result, Molly developed her own sensitivities and sensibilities. Before Steve and I moved to the property, I was acquainting our wandering cat to the perimeters. Surprisingly, the cat was a little fearful, very unlike her. Molly showed up, tail thrashing, happy to see me. I was about to give her a pet, when the possible crisis occurred to me of what those white teeth gnashing could do to my petite cat. My body tensed, and I froze. Molly immediately noted my fear, and gentled her happy steps, even looking embarrassed and apologetic!

Another drama happened when I drove out of my shop, using my new remote to lower my tall door, made to accommodate large equipment. Molly usually stood behind or beside my car whenever I was backing up, but this time she headed inside the shop to steal cat food. The door was lowering, and in my panic, I forgot that I could stop it mid-drop. I yelled at her to come. She ignored my call. I shouted louder, then emitted a high-pitched scream, which I didn't recognize coming out of me. Molly did, however. She trotted to me, looking sheepish and ashamed, as the door closed within ten inches of clearance.

A "command" she acquired with me was one she obeyed when I told her, "I'll take a kiss." She instantly responded with a white-toothed smile and not so sanitary lick.

Her road crossing became a great problem for everyone but her, it seemed. She would casually stop cars, and maybe it was intentional since they were probably speeding on our 35 mph road. The strangest and most dangerous was when snow remained on the road. An all-white dog lying in the middle of the road on snow covered asphalt was certain to cause concern. The knocks on the doors continued by conscientious travelers.

Her most outrageous, almost in-your-face challenge to traffic occurred the day that I was trimming a willow tree that had started growing too large in the ditch. We in the 'hood had a hard time seeing to pull out into traffic, so I took a saw out, standing almost on the road. I had only worked a few minutes when Molly saw me and came sauntering over. Nothing I said dissuaded her to stay off the road. She caused four cars to come to a complete stop. Uncaring, unafraid, and maybe leaving a message, she squatted directly on the already yellow line and peed. I think my eyes stuck higher in my head as my eyes rolled. My face turned red with embarrassment but I think Molly and I shared a little smirk for the usual speeders.

I guess all good dogs go to heaven, and her demise was not her daily dangerous jaunts across the road, but her desire for visiting some of her favorite people. She was used to climbing a neighbor's fence with ease when she was younger, but the horror came one afternoon as she climbed it, caught her leg, and dangled for a moment, while yelping screams came from the usually tough, pain oblivious dog. She never completely recovered, but continued her visitations more slowly.

Her acupuncture was ineffective because her spine and joints had become far too stiff.

When she was euthanized after sleeping on a tarp that filled a living room, to prevent urine and feces from seeping into the carpet, three of us were with her, her owners and I, plus the two veterinarians who came to her home. Our neighborhood has not been the same without our loving, intrepid Molly.

Baby Fox

A kit came to my pond last night to die. It was unfoxlike and more catlike the way she climbed the boulders above the pond, delicately, yet deliberately, to gaze into the water like a tiny child longing to float her toy sailboat one more time. She was 2/3 the size of her siblings and appeared alone. After looking in the water for mere moments, she climbed off the boulders to lie curled on the cool grass, her tail circled around her nose.

We love our foxes in my neighborhood, and we all feel horrible when one dies or disappears, but none were as devastated as Dee this time, whose side yard in which the adults chose to live, was a visual nature lesson as she watched through her screened window to see the mother nurse 4 kits, the father bringing occasional food and the kits playing in her grandchildren's play area. When danger seemed eminent, they could run down a culvert that started in her area.

Then came the day when the foxes were blamed for killing all of one neighbor's chickens. The owner told Dee he was going to live trap the mother, but wouldn't tell her what he would do with her after that. Dee tried to convince him that the kits would then die without her care, but he seemed unmoved. In a frantic effort to move the foxes to another area, Dee sprinkled coyote urine granules in the play area. When the mother returned to the play area, she stiffened, ears twitching. She nervously called out the kits for one last nursing before she separated them into 2 groups of 2. There was a lot of crying and calling out from the babies for a couple of nights, Dee's not the least of them. The foxes had been unfairly blamed we found out later; coyotes were the destructive ones.

Some of the young foxes in the litter moved across the street to play on the rocks in a house that would be rented. The new renters had 2 dogs that naturally chased the foxes. Dee believes that this baby who gave my pond and rocks a visit was temporarily caught in a fence while escaping and never completely recovered.

While the kit was lying by my pond, I took out some rotis-serie chicken to set on the ground and went to the shop for a few minutes. I had never seen this baby, nor its mother before, although a different female fox was becoming friendly with me in my yard. When I returned from the shop, the mother had appeared, snagged the chicken and ran toward a road in our neighborhood. I found the kit stretched out and dead. Had the mother killed the baby out of mercy? I haven't found the answer.

My neighbor Dee and I had trouble sleeping that night. "Nature is so cruel," she texted the next morning.

We feel privileged to have seen the foxes and to have them trust us, but the exit is cruelly painful.

Buffy

To be tamed by a feral animal is a journey into another realm of communication and honor. Buffy (Baby Mommy) was a tiny tabby born in our barn, probably sister to Samurai, with an outdoor feral awareness that disallowed receiving pets outside the barn until she was seven years old- an awareness that kept her alive for thirteen years. The Humane Society and I couldn't quite keep up with her child bearing. She had litter after litter, sometimes two a season, and shamelessly raised her rear to show her readiness toward all males in the neighborhood, and unabashedly reared litters which were sometimes the product of incest; her sons were as welcome as any in her wanton whoredom. But to label her as a whore would be to wrest away the dignity and gentleness that she showed her feral family.

When Steve and others began to have battles for settling the family estate, we had lived on the trout farm twenty-seven years, but needed to protect ourselves financially and emotionally, and bought a home in Weld County. The thought of leaving this lovely place, our home that we had poured our hearts and souls into without thanks or recognition was almost more than we could bear. Our sanity could only be saved by throwing ourselves into the hard work of beautifying our new home. Part of the permission to leave the Boulder place would be that Buffy, my oldest, sweetest cat would no longer be around.

In springtime, I had wiped Buffy's watery eyes every morning, sometimes wiping the color of blood from her running eyes. When one frightening morning I found the membrane of her left eye covering a third of her eyeball, I knew I needed to take her to the vet.

When I explained that she was feral, the receptionist told me that she would need to be anesthetized in order for the vet to have a look. She asked how old she was and I told her at least eleven. She asked in surprise, "And she's still feral?" Very few people who had a barn full of cats surrounded by coyotes and ill-mannered neighborhood dogs would ask such a question. When she asked if Buffy were spayed, I told her no. She told me that while Buffy was anesthetized, they would spay her. I panicked, knowing that spaying could be the cause of her death. They would have it no other way at the Boulder Humane Society. I didn't want her to go blind either, which would have been her death sentence as well, so I agreed.

When I live trapped Buffy, she panicked at first, tried to climb the top wires, then appeared defeated, as if she knew she had done something very stupid and deadly.

When I was in the patient room, the vet entered to deal with my concerns: "She may be thirteen years old," I told her. " Will a spay job exacerbate her eye problem?"

Dr. Leslie looked at Buffy through the wires of the live trap.

"Is she scared?"

"Terrified," I replied.

"I don't need to examine your cat," she said gently. "She may have a brain tumor or other idiosyncratic ailment causing the membrane to cover her eye. You could just take her home."

When I shook her hand and thanked her with a quavering voice, she couldn't have known all that Buffy's reprieve had meant to me; I wouldn't be forced to move-I wasn't given the permission to do so.

Catwalk

Hark, Hark, the dogs do bark;
Somebody's walking a cat in the park!

Those lines, quipped by an unremembered comedian, stuck me as hilarious when I was in high school. How could I have known how prophetic they would be as I traveled regularly from Colorado to Nebraska, taking my cat along because I'm sure she would miss me terribly if she ever deigned to notice I was gone?

This 8# 2oz lady wrestler, strong-willed as a water buffalo at a buffet in an all-inclusive hotel, prefers to work alone, her way. She could turn a 15 minute pit stop along the journey into a two hour mouse harassment event, ensuring the poor mouse could never have grandchildren. When she doesn't feel she needs to cooperate on her leash, she will flip over, attempting to entangle it in her harness. If I pull her along on her side, she'll pull out of her harness....a planned retaliation. If that doesn't suit her, she's sure to force out a whine and pretend to attack.

She showed up at our place in Nebraska as a half grown kitten, skin and bones and loaded with ticks. She was extremely friendly then, so happy to be rescued, but now that she has the control, she's rather arrogant, even ungrateful; a princess, bedecked in jewels that other cats seem to see and respect.

I believe it's her attitude that transfers unspoken sassy retorts into my mind when people comment about our leash and harness act. Things like: "Wow! I never seen a cat on a leash before!" might lead to a response such as: "Yeah, well I hoped I wouldn't a heerd bad grammar after I retired from my illustrious career as an English teacher."

A grinning trucker at a rest stop stood and stared at us, making his little yapping dawgs gawk as well. Mitten glared back, back arched. She was always irritated at little dogs.. big dogs too. Medium dogs…

Yet another sighting involved two giggling Mexican brothers who couldn't stop staring. Mitten let that one go. I think she thought they were cute.

We were both startled by a tree bashing sound emitted from the park beside a golf course in North Platte. It turned out to be a guy emerging from the stand of trees, multiple golf balls in hand. He stopped and looked with some disinterest, stating that he'd never seen a cat on a leash before. My barely controlled retort was: "Yeah, well I've never seen anyone fool enough to crash through stickery cedars, just to shag a few balls to save a buck."

Then there was the lady from Tennessee who stood and studied our match up.

"Is that a ca at?" she drawled, turning a one-syllable word into two long ones.

"No, I'm a Chihuahua/Rottweiler mix. Please be cautious."

Mitten knows she has the control now. If she were to see this short story, she would laugh scornfully, knowing that she's the one dragging me along on my leash.

Loki

When one adopts a pet without knowing its background, there is continual work toward mystery solving, pieced together by observable bits of behavior. Such is the case with Loki, my friends' "ravenous" cat. Why is this well fed cat continuously feeling the need to steal bites and leftovers of other cats? Why does he seek the favorable attention of other cats so unfavorably? He would often turn a friendly nose touch or paw and arm slung over my cat Splish, into a back smack or head slap. Why, when it was obvious he was in love with the coy Mitten, would he rush the moment, causing the arrogant princess to yowl in protest and pretended pain?

The answer appeared to me with perfect clarity on a Tuesday morning. I arose earlier than usual, and went out to feed Splish, my cat, in the shop when I saw Loki and Splish sitting companionably together by the ditch under the little bridge. This friendly acceptance had been happening more recently, but this time they were intent on the hunt. Both were patiently watching for the mouse to move in the tall grass. Splish was a disciplined hunter, sometimes out of necessity back on the farm in Boulder, where he allowed kittens to eat his share of cat food. Loki in no way demonstrated this concentration. He turned his head to watch me approach the shop. Turning back to wait for the mouse, he was again distracted by a flock of geese flying overhead. Doing his best to concentrate again, he snapped his head my way as I unlocked the shop. His mind seemed to be thinking: "Work for this meal, or snag an easy one?"

Puzzle solved!! Loki had ADFD! My neighbors had adopted a Special Needs cat! His overeating was a reaction to his social rejection from his overzealous approach to friendship. His attention deficit feline disorder was a seldom observed, rarely studied syndrome that affected misunderstood cats. Thus, placing cats on special weight loss diets is ineffective. What they need is just to be understood by their new owners, given some slack and accepted into the world of cat.

Tough Calf

I went out to pet the calf. It was lying in a lean-to shed within a pen, but when I approached the railing, it jumped up and ran to the opposite side of me, its nostrils blowing out fear. I took it personally since most calves would come for grain and maybe a little nuzzle, but then I rationalized its nervousness to the noise and active play the 7 cousins had been creating in the yard for a few hours.

I was at the Weld County farm and ranch of friends I'd had so long that I considered them 2nd family. After I'd gone inside, one of the relatives asked me if I'd seen the calf, and if I knew the story behind him. He and others there began to unravel the story behind the calf's fear, and pieced together a story that was a shockingly amazing story of survival.

The calf had been in on branding time in the summer, but after that time had disappeared for a period of time that extended to 5 months, living in a large pasture alone, eating grass that must have mainly just run through him, with his lacking the ruminant ability to aid his digestion for nourishment.

When the neighbor was rounding up his cattle, he found an undersized, malnourished calf with a brand unlike his own. He called my friend who rode his horse into the pasture. The calf that had battled to stay alive charged his horse! But then fell down! As a result, the calf was roped, tied and flung over the horse, thrashing all the way.

The calf, unused to people or other cattle, is in a pen by himself, fed a type of milk grain that is adding weight to his thin body.

The ranchers were amazed and saddened by the story they told, but seemed to know that the calf would fight to live and begin to thrive under their care. They named him Chance.

Jessie

I often equate the loss of our dog, Jessie, to the loss of our lake. We ran together with a joy and wildness in an area that has been overtaken by human fishing machines who feel no guilt about removing a bucketful of fish. The broken leg that never healed because it was never dealt with, nor her ear that never stood straight failed to slow her down or diminish her sense of freedom as we ran together. Both were the results of an abusive owner, from whom Bob, one of our workers, took Jessie, and in turn, I was unselfishly given her by Bob, because he saw how we connected with each other.

I never scolded Jessie because she always seemed to read my mind and considered me her true owner and mentor…..except once. We were running our usual route, when Jessie spotted a fox. When she gave chase, I tried continuously to call her back. She ignored me for ten minutes. When she finally returned, not appearing guilty, but instead, exhausted; she seemed unable to control her tongue which was lolling lengthily as she panted, trying to regain a little O2. I scolded her for the first time, raising my voice and shaking my finger at her, but abruptly stopped. As I looked up, I saw a figure appear: her friend, the fox, who had turned around to come to fetch Jessie, wondering where her new playmate had gone!

On the Fourth of July, Steve and I left town, relying on one of our workers to do chores, including taking care of Jessie. When we returned home Jessie was not there. Our worker had forgotten to feed her and put her in her doghouse. Steve found her body on Valmont, after she had been hit by a car, running from the noise and lights of fireworks. We buried her in the trench by the lake. The trespassers who walk by seem sacrilegious in not honoring her spirit.

I sometimes imagine my arms around her golden fur and picture her intelligent liquid brown eyes watching me with alertness and adoration, a look I may never see again.

Mitten Found Us

Mitten, our cat, found us. We had just arrived in Nebraska, and as we got out of the truck, I heard a muffled bang against metal, underneath a shipping container we used for yard tools. When we were finished hauling items into the house, we sat down on our deck to have a beer. We were chatting quietly, when something bumped against my leg. She must have decided we were approachable, and maybe we would even have food. She was an older kitten, skin and bones and full of ticks...fully engorged ones! When I offered her some pork fat not thrown out from lunch, she ignored it, and instead, stretched her emaciated body onto my leg to be picked up. After that bit of lovin', I offered her some cereal in milk, but she wasn't interested in that either.

We were determined not to have a house cat again. In the late afternoon, I took her to our shop and set her on my lap on a lawn chair. She was so exhausted in her run-down shape, she went to sleep almost immediately. I began to remove the multitude of greedy, blood-sucking ticks, and throw them into a bucket. The only time she gently protested, pushing my hand away was when instead of a tick, I was trying to remove a nipple!

I just couldn't give her away after being unable to find the owner, who must have lost her as she floated down the river in the tubes the outfitters rented. After these thirteen years, I'm not giving her back!

Mitten Was Bitten in Her Tail

Mitten, our cat, was bitten in that extremely sensitive area above her tail, by a neighbor cat. It was such a painful spot that when she cleaned it, she would gargle a cry and run away from her tail.

The "Youts"

My Cousin Vinny

"Is it possible the two youts……,"
asked Vinny in "My Cousin Vinny".

"The two what?" asked Judge Chamberlain Haller.
"What was that word? What is a yout?"

"Oh, excuse me, Your Honor. The two de Fen dants."

Yadira

"Joe, we need to pick up Yadira. It's the third time this week she's missed my first hour."

I was talking to Joe Martinez, my school's assistant principal about doing a home visitation to "persuade" Yadira to better attendance. Many families with students at our school didn't have phones, most parents worked outside the home, and, in general, it was difficult to contact them. Added to other attendance problems was the fact that our school district no longer put money into enforcing the mandatory attendance until 16-years-old law, and although it was never spoken, many 7-12th grade drop-outs and slide-outs had been testing its limits.

Yadira, the A student/F student, the ditcher, the kid with imperfect attendance, the 7th grader with an adult sense of humor, the girl who was as tall as she was round, was causing me some frustration I had little time to address. Many things were disappointing me regarding Yadira. This year her ditching, obviously, but the year before she had failed the 7th grade, even though she was very bright and a good reader. I really think she liked enough of her 7th grade teachers to not mind seeing them for another year. In addition, she was lazy. Her attendance the year before had been sporadic.

One day when she showed up on a gray, drizzling afternoon for her first class of the day, she told me that she had awakened and, seeing the rain, had thought, "It's a good day for sleeping." She had pulled the covers to her neck and rolled over. She had told me that her mother often threatened to get her out of bed the hard way. She finally made Yadira a believer on a day when el sol didn't shine. Yadira had rolled over to snooze a little longer. She had awakened slightly, reaching for her covers which little by little were moving away from her. When they reached the foot of the bed, the glass of water that had been set there by her mother, tipped, spilling its contents over Yadira's feet, finally causing her to climb out of bed. She made it to school the next day.

Yadira's lack of attendance was particularly disturbing to me because the year before, I had recognized some of her dramatic talents, and though her school work was often mediocre, I asked her to tell a "Cuento" (short story), at the multi-cultural festival in the town that housed our district office. She chose the longest story of all the students who would tell stories, "The Million Dollar Somersaults". She never missed a practice, and her story was memorized first with all the actions and wit that came so naturally to Yadira.

On the day of the festival, she showed up 15 minutes early as directed. (No sleeping in that day.) I introduced two well-known Hispanics in the town: one was a banker and city councilman; the other, the president of El Comite, an action and information dissemination and clearing house group.

The first of the two told the story of his climb to fame from an itinerant farmer's son to City Councilman. He spoke to me only; we had no audience. It was early in the festival and the outdoor puppet show and Tai-Kwondo demos were drawing the interest of the crowd. The woman from El Comite played her guitar and sang, and told the story of La Llarona, a classic favorite about a ghost lady who steals children. Her only audience was her son and daughter, and even they left in the middle of her song, drawn by the outdoor activities.

When it was the students' turn to tell their cuentos, family members began wandering in, which drew others, and the travel agency room we had been loaned began to fill.

I strategically placed Yadira's story in the middle….two shorts, one long, two shorts, would hold an audience for 45 minutes. I had told the organizer of the entire storytelling section of the festival that she needed to show up at 10:15 for the treat of seeing Yadira act out the story. She wasn't disappointed.

Yadira's lovely mother had shown up. She spoke no English and my limited Spanish didn't seem to put her at ease, but anyone could see the pride she felt for her daughter. With her was Yadira's 3-year-old half- brother, a beautiful curly-haired, husky boy with eyelashes that could have set him into flight if he blinked fast enough.

At last it was Yadira's turn. It seems trite and usually untrue to say that a person's body is as round as it is tall, but in her case, it was almost true. Her egg-shape was met with slightly knock-knees with dimples that had impish grins on them saying, "I like this bod just fine!" Her poodle-curled hair sat tightly upon her head. Her eyes were deep-set and intelligent, warning of surprises coming our way.

I introduced Yadira, and she began her tale. The smiles of the audience increased as her brother ran to embrace her knees, and cling to her for the duration of the cuento, with Yadira not missing a beat.

The story was of a poor Mexican girl who had lost her parents and went to live with an important, wealthy uncle in Spain. She was given a different dress to wear each day with matching fans and hats with Yadira acting out the part of fanning herself delicately.

The little girl became so enamored with herself that she felt she was too good for all the other little girls except for a princess. Her uncle saw this and at his time of death the stipulations of his will stated that she would have to call the townspeople to the main plaza and perform 3 somersaults in front of them to inherit his money.

When it was time for the somersaults, our crowd waited as expectantly as the crowd in the plaza in the story for Yadira to roll across the floor. She only partially disappointed them when she dipped slightly, pretending to begin a somersault, then instead drew laughs by telling them that the little girl's dress came over her head, showing her little pantalones. The little girl was so humiliated that she cried, gaining the compassion of the crowd in the plaza, including the little girls she had snubbed.

When Yadira was finished, she drew hearty applause. Her mother was proudly embarrassed. Yadira had shown the confident poise of an experienced actress. She was a success, as was the festival.

The school year ended with Yadira asking to tell a cuento the next year. She would drop by my classroom after school to chat and make humorous observations with her adult-like sense of humor. She sometimes graded papers for me, but was careless and disinterested in turning in her own work.

When the next school year began, I found Yadira had been placed again in my first hour English class. First hour was a tough class to attend for a sleeping girl, unmotivated to crawl out from under dry covers.

By third quarter of the following year I had told Yadira that I wasn't organizing the cuentos presentations that year. She was beginning to miss 2 or 3 classes a week again in my first hour. My assistant principal brought Luis, Yadira's older brother, along as we climbed into Joe's car to speak to Yadira's parents. Luis was a well-rounded student. He made the honor roll quarter after quarter. He was a junior varsity quarterback, and a gifted basketball player. He was unaware that Yadira had been missing so much school. He knew that she and her 16-year-old sister got up in the morning, got ready for school, and drove away together in Nayeli's car.

We arrived at a somnolent house. Both parents worked night shifts, and 9:30 a.m. was their nighttime. Angelically asleep on the couch in yellow sleepers with his exquisite lashes feathering his cheeks, was the baby half-brother who had "assisted" with Yadira's storytelling; he was so peaceful, I wanted to join him on the couch and forget about school problems.

Luis awakened his mother who came out groggily concerned. She, too, was unaware of Yadira's ditching. She and Joe spoke Spanish as I tried to catch words and phrases. Neither Yadira nor Nayeli were at home or at school, but 20 minutes after we returned, Yadira showed up during the passing period. Her locker was across from my room. She wouldn't look at me or speak to me. When I made a joking comment to her, she raised her head slightly, the better to ignore me. This attitude continued for 2 weeks, but her attendance was perfect.

Finally, one morning in the hallway, things seemed instantly back to normal. That's the way middle school kids are: they usually can't hold a grudge against a teacher too long; it takes too much energy.

Yadira was looking at a girl down the hall who was constantly the instigator or involved in nearly every girl fight or argument that existed in 7th grade.

"Mrs. Cline, what would you do if I went up to Rachel and punched her in the face?"

Knowing Yadira wasn't a fighter or troublemaker, I answered:

"I'd probably whistle and look the other way."

Things became ok between us.

My last written assignment was one regarding an experience that had some meaning to them, one that changed their lives in some way. Yadira wrote about hearing an argument in their driveway. When she went out, she saw that it was her biological father and her mother shouting at each other. Her father wanted custody of the 3 kids after not seeing them for years. Yadira wrote in her paper that she hated him for his desertion and for wishing to interfere with the step-father who was more a father to her than the "real" father had ever been. She ended with, "When it was my turn to speak in court, I had my chance to tell him." It was by far the best paper she had ever written, and one of the best in the 7th grade.

On the last day of school for the year, I said my parting words to each of my classes, and Yadira stayed after class for a moment to slip a folded note into my hand.

It said: Mrs. Cline,

I just wrote to say thanks for going to my house and everything you did. I realize it was for my own good! I'm glad there are teachers like you who care about their students.

Thank you,

Your biggest headache,

Yadira

p.s.

Please don't show this to any other student. I have a rep. to care for.

Betty in My House

My father is a very calm person. He should have been a fireman. However, when an alarm went off, he would have finished his hand of gin, replaced the cards in the deck, donned an asbestos suit and, after checking the polish on the engine, he could wait until the Dalmatian mascot's puppies were six weeks old, gather them all together and sell them on the way to the fire, stopping only to get change at the bank for large bills. This method would save needless panic at fires and eliminate costly detailed home repair bills. The house would, of course, have been burned to the ground by the time he arrived, but it would save insurance adjusters' headaches.

Anyway, my father's not a fireman; he's an insurance adjuster. He used to get upset when people whose houses burned weren't satisfied with his adjusting. He used to roar at them, and then he would come home and roar at us. Those were the only times I saw (and heard) him mad. Then he found an effective method for remaining calm. When they were arguing about the insurance payout, my father would light his cigarette with a lighter that had about a four inch flame. That too-close-for-comfort fire made them a little jumpy and Father's job a little easier. Father got so calm about everything that he actually started to feel sorry for the fools who smoked in bed, didn't repair frayed electrical wiring and in general, were walking fire hazards.

He knew this family whose home burned. Although they weren't really friends, he asked them to dinner. They had a daughter about my age.

I helped Mother fix dinner that night. It wasn't my idea, but we made spaghetti and broccoli almondine. What a way to welcome guests! First they could die of embarrassment when their spaghetti unwound into their laps, and then they could throw up their broccoli or pick out the almonds so Mother would think they were eating something. Mother wore her good black dress. I told her not to because it would probably remind them of charcoal. She forced me to wear some stupid dress she bought me. She really brought home some taste killers at times.

My father answered the door, slapped Mr. Bates on the back, damn near making him slip a disc. He kissed Mrs. Bates's hand after bowing to her. He was a real prince that night. Mrs. Bates just blushed, giggled and nodded. They came in, and who should be straggling behind but their daughter, Betty, the Frog Princess. Boy, she was really bad. She had on high white sport socks, and I think they were so white they were almost phosphorescent! Then she had on a dress, and it was ten times more embarrassing than the one I had on. My mother and she should go shopping together! To top it all off, the weirdo had on these curling, spiraling cat-eye glasses. When they introduced her, she didn't even bother to smile or even react. At least I could flash some teeth when I had to. She just ignored everyone and looked at the table. Her father gave her a little reminder thwack on the back of her head.

"Say hello to Mr. and Mrs. Stevens."

"Hello to Mr. and Mrs. Stevens."

The thwack was swift and immediate on her left cheek, leaving a slight red mark. The look on Mr. Bates' face was one of shockingly instant rage, quickly replaced by an embarrassed, apologetic smile to my parents. Betty's eyes watered, nearly camouflaged by her outdated glasses.

"Hello, Mr. and Mrs. Stevens. Pleased to make your acquaintances," Betty responded hoarsely, hoping she would get away with her not so subtle form of sarcasm.

We all sat around for a while until dinner was ready. Betty the Beauty kept looking around at our furniture, everything in our china cabinet and the goblets on the table. After she had looked at all that, she always ended up looking at my feet. Then she'd go through the whole cycle again. I really hated people who stared at feet, so when she looked again, I pointed my toes together so that I looked severely pigeon-toed, enough to be debilitated. Betty looked at my face to see if I were kidding, but I pretended I was listening to my father.

When she looked at my feet again, I crossed my legs and wound them around each other twice, like Olive Oyl in Popeye cartoons. I think she caught on this time and quit staring. She looked pretty mad. When we sat down to eat, she hardly said anything. I couldn't blame anyone for that, though.

Mr. Bates talked hurriedly, pausing to take a forkful of food, then chattering away, sometimes with his mouth open, exposing the bite of food he had just helped himself to.

"Thank you for having us for dinner, Mr. and Mrs. Stevens. We appreciate it. We're all three anxious about our move to another place, be it another house, town, city or state. We just can't decide where and what or who could accommodate us. I have to tell you that we have a lot of problems as a family: my daughter doesn't do well in school with academics and has social issues as well." I was embarrassed for Betty as Mr. Bates talked about her as if she wasn't there. I saw the slightest flash of an angry glare toward her father, which turned into such a look of hate that I sucked in my breath.

"My wife, as you can see, is painfully shy and probably unqualified for any job, since she doesn't have no…..any real skills or education for working outside the home. Her parents didn't trust the educational system." Mrs. Bates just sat there and acted the way Mr. Bates described her, not adding to the conversation. She looked down at her hands as she squeezed them together, keeping her head bowed as she nervously rubbed each finger in order.

"I think I can retain my job so far, but rental prices keep climbing and becoming unaffordable for a family. I'm at my wits' end trying to put this all together. "

"What can you do for us, Mr. Stevens…….Jack?" he asked abruptly.

My father was hardly ever caught off guard, but Mr. Bates had surprised him with his directness. I knew he and Mother felt sorry for them, and after a little silent signal between them, they excused themselves to talk in the kitchen.

I felt strange and oh so alone, feeling that I needed to entertain the Bates family, but they seemed to have their own silent conversations with each other, consisting of Mr. Bates making a fist and subtly shaking it at Betty, while Mrs. Bates looked at her husband with pleading eyes.

When my parents returned, both of them graciously asked the Bates family to stay with us until such time as they had a more permanent residence.

"Well," I thought, "Nobody asked me!" But it was fun getting the guest rooms ready. My mother and I worked well together, and surprisingly, even Mrs. Bates helped with dusting the furniture. Betty just stood there like she was daring us to ask her to help out.

After we finished up the guest rooms, I told Mother I had some homework. She probably would have made me entertain Betty if I hadn't made up something. I could have left my feet in the room and kept her occupied for three or four days though.

Betty and I had to share the bathroom off of my room. I was reading in bed and Betty came traipsing through my room in these flannel pajamas with cars or something stupid on them. She had her glasses off and she had giant cow eyes that reminded me of my grandfather's cow, Flossie. I decided to be friendly.

"How's it going, Flossie?"

She ignored me. When she came out of the bathroom, I told her I hoped she would have a pleasant stay.

"Well, I won't."

Of all the girls whose houses burn, I had to get one with a nasty personality.

We went to the same middle school, so I had to walk with her to school. Our conversations were really interesting since she enunciated her yes's and no's very well. On the way to school we met my best friend, Brenda. Brenda got a little bored with Betty's non-conversations too. We ignored her after a few seconds of that. Brenda's boyfriend walked her home from school on Fridays, so I rode my bike on those days. Everybody at school made fun of me a lot for riding it, but Fridays were my bicycle days, so screw them.

One Friday I was speeding along the sidewalk, and I saw Betty walking ahead of me, so I speeded up and passed her and stopped so that she ran into my bike. I really laid a patch! She didn't even laugh so I asked her if she wanted to ride on the front of my bike. She was pretty offended when she saw I didn't have a fender.

A few nights later at dinner she actually said something. It was only, "Pass the carrots," but then it nearly killed me when she said, "Thank you."

That night she came into my room and started telling me about this science project she was going to do. I'd never seen her so excited. It was all about these little white mice, and she was building a maze. I really couldn't believe her eyes could get much bigger, but they really did. All I could think of was Flossie, the cow, having a calf or wearing a cold milking machine. I didn't know she could talk, let alone rattle on for five minutes. She asked me if I thought she should do that for her project. I told her if she wouldn't be embarrassed, I wouldn't be. I had to do a report, so I told her to go away because she was bugging me. She shut up right away and just gawked at me. The cow eyes turned to bloodhound eyes. She grabbed her half-built maze and left. She didn't even come back that night to mess up my bathroom. During the night I got up to go to the bathroom, and saw Mr. Bates leaving Betty's bedroom, making a dedicated effort to tiptoe. I heard a little whimper in the room and wondered if they had sneaked a puppy in.

That morning she left for school earlier than I did. After school I waited for her, but she had already left. When I got home I went to dump my books in my room and there was a fire on my dresser. I rushed into the bathroom, got a wet washcloth and threw it on the fire. It was only a little alcohol fire, but I was pretty mad. Obviously I needed to deal with Betty, and I was going to rush in and snap her to death with the washcloth unless she confessed, but I decided to trick her into confessing and apologizing.

We had a set of Great Books and one of them was on Sigmund Freud. I couldn't find anything about fires, just dreams, mainly. I kept the book under my bed to read the next day. Every time I went toward my room, I would play Private Eye. I'd flatten myself against the wall and slide along, looking both ways and peek into my room. It was very dramatic. That night when she went through my room into the bathroom, I looked her over for matches, but she didn't have any that I could see. When she was in the bathroom, I ran into her room to get some clues. She had matches on her dresser. I got a notebook and wrote, "Clues" on the first page and under that I wrote, "Matches on dresser."

I wanted to get some track shoes so I could zip into the bathroom to see if there were any towels on fire. I was bent over ready to peek under the door, when she came out and bumped my head with the door. Nothing was burning. I felt like a real hero defending both places at once. I had one foot in each room until she was in her room. I knew I'd wake up that night engulfed in flames. I'd feel like a real martyr crawling between anything flammable.

The next day I came back from school and started reading the book on Sigmund Freud. I read that dreams were an unconscious form of wish fulfillment. That night when Betty came through my room, I asked her if she had dreamed anything lately.

"I don't dream."

"Everybody dreams."

"I don't."

"Oh, come on. I bet you dreamed last night."

"Ok, I dreamed I was a torch bearer raiding and looting villages."

She went into the bathroom and I got out my notebook.

I wrote: "Dreams about being a torch bearer."

That night something woke me up. When I went out to the hall to check it out, I saw Mr. Bates holding Betty's head back with a grip on her hair.

"No Dad, please.......don't!"

He was half dragging, half frog-marching her into her room, clumsily trying to clap a hand over her mouth, then shutting the door quickly.

I didn't know what to tell my father, since I didn't really understand what I saw, but I knew he would figure things out.

The next day after school I was sliding along the wall, and I peeked into my room, and there was Betty throwing a match into alcohol. I really hadn't expected to catch her. All the wall sliding was just a game. Finding her was so surprising that I screamed. She hadn't expected to be caught in the act either, and she screamed. We had a real chorus going. I tackled her and started pounding her. Then I decided to put out the fire. She went into her room. After I got the fire out I went into her room too.

"What are you trying to do?"

She didn't answer me. I asked her again and started pounding her.

"I don't have to talk to you."

"I don't have to tell your mother either, but I'm going to."

"Go ahead."

"I'll probably tell your FATHER!" At that, the blood left her face, leaving her pale and a little breathless.

"Go ahead," she said shakily, without conviction.

I didn't tell either parent. I decided she was messed up enough without her mother and especially her father screaming at her. I had a feeling that she wouldn't start any more fires.

When I told my father that Mr. Bates was being really mean to Betty, and told him what I had witnessed, he got this look on his face of bewilderment, rage and disgust that I had never seen before. The next day it seemed that Dad and Mr. Bates had a little discussion in Dad's office. Mr. Bates came out of there pale, his mouth opening and shutting like a fish left on the bank, gasping for air.

The Bates family left the next day to some place six hundred miles away, or so Mr. Bates told my father. They didn't leave a forwarding address. I couldn't say that it was quieter; there wasn't much noise when Betty was here, but my nervousness disappeared, along with the unexplained things I saw Mr. Bates do that I didn't really understand.

Mother and I cleaned Betty's room with what we thought was a thorough job of changing linens, polishing the furniture and spot cleaning the carpet. A week later though, a rotten smell started creeping out of the room. When we investigated under the mattress, we found eight white mice with their heads smashed in.

Teenage Girls Turned Loose

When I was fifteen and living on a farm thirty miles from Greeley, Colorado, seventeen miles south of Briggsdale, where I went to high school, with the closest neighbor five miles away (who was a bachelor lots older than fifteen), I had to make creative use of socialization time.

The whole event started the summer weekend my friend, Sandy, was staying with me. Our house wasn't built yet, and our family of four was living in close quarters in a mobile home. Our hired man, Mike, was staying in our Quonset which was basically a large metal garage for farm machinery. He had a single bed set up by the east wall of his 2,000 square foot bedroom. He didn't need to decorate with posters of vehicles- he was surrounded by the real things. His night stand was an upright set of plow discs which held his alarm clock and a small transistor radio. Below the top shelf were the curved discs which held nuts and bolts. His closet and shelf was an upraised tractor bucket.

Mike was ready to begin his sophomore year of college. He was muscular and cute. The only thing even slightly marring his good looks was a glass eye which he had obtained after playing a little farm game with his brother called, "Tag around the haystack with BB guns."

The action began with a steak dinner which mom cooked and Sandy and I rushed through. We didn't need to spend time savoring our steaks- we were farms girls; we had it most nights.

With the sun threatening to set, Sandy and I were lucky to ever find the lizard. I never could remember if we first thought of finding a lizard or if it came looking for us to give us the idea. We caught the willing lizard and began to formulate our plan.

There were four sets of windows on the Quonset, two on the north and two south.

"Wouldn't it be funny?" we thought, "to put the lizard into Mike's bed, peek through the window and watch him panic and leap out, and maybe even bump his head on the tractor bucket, or knock over the nuts and bolts, and maybe even step on them so we could see how well he can dance?"

"That would be hilarious!" we decided.

We didn't know how much time we had, but the sun was rapidly going down, and for a farmer in summer, that meant bedtime. It wouldn't be long before Mike would be coming to his bedroom garage!

We gently tucked the lizard into Mike's bed, placing him at the foot of the bed to make him less squashable.

The windows of the Quonset were high so we needed a platform. We found a pile of cinder blocks and began stacking. We ended with a two and a half feet high double stack for Sandy and one for me. It was time for the test. We both had a little trouble stepping high enough to reach the top of the stacks without causing them to shift, and we found ourselves leaning on each other for some shaky support. When we were finally in place, we could see inside the Quonset with the fading rays of the sun-a perfect vantage point for our clever, devious plan.

We waited. We waited some more. Nerves finally got to Sandy, and she informed me that if she didn't run to the bathroom right then, she would wet her pants.

"This is the country, remember? Play like a farmer and go by a tree!"

She said ok, but as she was ready to jump down from our cinder-block balcony, I heard Mike coming.

"Here he comes!" I whisper-yelled at her.

"I have to pee!" she seethed back.

"Just toughen up!"

It was too good a show to miss.

Mike pushed open the long Quonset doors and walked toward his bed. He set down what was probably his shaving kit, and, as we had hoped, turned on the flashlight he had on his makeshift nightstand.

After a moment of trying to find a radio station in the non-receptive steel building, he gave up and sat down on his bed, not yet turning back the covers.

Giggles bubbled up inside of Sandy and me, and then abruptly, Mike stood up and started taking off his shirt! I had forgotten about this part! Now I was going to watch a great joke happen, and watch a cute guy take off his clothes too! What a bonus!

I think that part of the plan had eluded Sandy as well, because by the time he had his shirt off and was going for the belt, I heard a big gasp come out of her. She grabbed for me as her vibrations caused her blocks to shift dramatically, and as she did, I fell against the corrugated steel of the Quonset, causing what seemed like an explosive sound. I only had time to catch a glimpse of Mike catching a glimpse of me before all hell broke loose.

Sandy and I were both on the ground with cinder blocks in great disarray. Sandy told me that she really was wetting her pants. Mike must have been yelling pretty loudly to be heard above the grinding sound of the collapsing blocks, but I could tell he was on the move toward the doors, shouting something to the effect of catching us both at once and smacking both our butts.

"Have fun spanking Sandy's," I thought.

I ran like a streak, and Sandy ran like wet lightening, until we found the safety of some farm machinery. We crouched down and waited to be found and killed or at least pounded. We waited, hoping our hearts would stop pounding so that we could finally hear. I was sure that Mike was playing Indian and would sneak up on us quietly so that I would wet my pants too, so I was doing the crouching duck walk, turning every few seconds.

Finally, all sound died away except for the crickets rubbing their legs together in amused applause for our performance.

"Do you hear him?" Sandy whispered.

"No, but that doesn't mean he's not out here."

After ten minutes of waiting, we decided we would rather be beat to death than die of boredom, so we abandoned our refuge. We walked across the yard waiting to be jumped, but- no Mike. We walked the full length of the seventy-five yards back to the trailer, but Mike didn't appear for his revenge. When we arrived inside, I really thought Sandy needed to hit the shower before bedtime.

The next day Mike and my dad went to work early. Sandy and I slept late, and then Mom and I took her home. I really didn't want her to run out of clothes and have to borrow mine while she was here, what with the things she did to then. I really hadn't thought about the lizard again, so apparently, it had crawled out on its own, without discovery.

I didn't see Mike until dinner. I was nervously expecting our episode to be a hot topic over the roast beef, but conversation skirted that issue. Then I thought that Mike was so bent on revenge that he had really made the story an exaggeration, and that I would have to be spoken to alone by my parents.

After dishes were finished, Mom was finishing up in the kitchen, Dad had gone outside, and Mike and I were in the living room watching TV. Mike said my name.

I thought, "Here it comes!"

I said, "What?" too embarrassed to look at him.

"Look!" he said.

When I looked, Mike had his glass eye in his hand, and pretended to be cleaning it.

"Gross!" I squealed, turning my head away.

Mike laughed gleefully, and I knew that was my punishment; he hadn't told my parents, probably never would, and all was forgiven.

He went to college that fall; we saw him only occasionally, and then not at all.

Two years later we had built our house and Mike's brother Kevin (pronounced Keevun, probably after his father whose name was Gerald, but pronounced Gairold; we could spell out there in the boondocks, we just couldn't pronounce.) Anyway, his brother Kevin was working for my father. My sister and I had our own bedrooms. My own PRIVATE domain- my impregnable fortress!

One evening, however, as I was going to bed, my domain had been violated! I crawled into bed, shrieked, and leaped out! A lizard went scuttling under my bed.

There was a knock on my door.

When I answered it, Kevin was there with an over-sized grin on his face.

"Did you find the lizard?" he asked.

"Yes! Stay out of my room!"

"Mike says, 'Hi'", he smiled.

Angela, Just one of the Guys, But Smarter

When I was ten everyone thought I was a precocious little girl. I guess the word got around because of Mrs. De Saab, the Gossip Gazette of our town. It all started when the old bat was visiting my mother. I was reading my horoscope and I told my mother that I'd better walk softly and carry a big stick because today I would reach the point where I would want to express my ideas, hopes and wishes, but if I told all, I would miss bargaining points for the future when I would really need them.

"What a precocious child!" Mrs. De Saab said, turning two backward somersaults in her chair and hitching up her bra strap. I don't think I was too precocious, though. My father said walk softly and all that a lot, so I just picked it up from him. Besides, I really believed in horoscopes then. Besides all that, I didn't even know what precocious meant. I thought since it came from Mrs. De Saab, it probably meant I had a growth on my neck or something. It took me about an hour to look it up.

I wanted to join the boys' baseball team in the summer, so I started to save my measly allowance (fifty cents a week) for a mitt. I was pretty ugly even with my long hair, but I thought I'd need it short to be on the team, so I put my father's overcoat on a chair, crawled under a desk and pulled the chair after me so Mother couldn't find me. That scissors and I sometimes didn't agree, and when I came out and took a look in the mirror, I thought an orphan had come to visit. There were patches about a half inch long that wouldn't stay down even with water. I had to wear my father's Butch Wax for a while, but the guys told me it would spring up in class anyway. I wanted a crew cut like my father's but my mother decided it was certainly short enough the way it was. I had to beat up about three guys that week because of my hair.

After my second fight one recess, I was on my way to the fort the guys and I had built when Mary Sue McCarthy came running at me like she had a cob up her butt.

"Hey Angie! Wanna play dolls?"

I couldn't believe the damn sissy. She had a lot of nerve alright.

"Play with that stupid rag?"

I grabbed that doll from her and kicked it about a mile down the playground. Its head fell off and rolled about a mile farther. I thought that girl was having an attack! She was crying so hard that she could hardly breathe. She kept telling me I broke her doll. You'd have thought it was her own damn plastic flesh! It got pretty sickening after about four hours and I gave her a big clout on her damn mouth. It shut her up for about a second, and then it started all over again. Recess time was going fast so I ran like the wind like the fox in my Reader, stopped on a dime and picked up the stupid doll. I started screwing Sally's head back and finally got it on. It was backwards, but recess was no time to mess around. I finally got to the fort.

Since I was the woman I sometimes made mudballs for the guys. I only made them for the guys I liked, and I liked them all pretty well when they gave me money. One guy, Billy John Raefert, never paid me. He was always the last one to be picked for the fort teams. I felt kind of sorry for him, but he didn't exactly command my respect if you know what I mean. He only had two shirts and he had to wear each one for a week before his mother would let him change. His shoes were those wrinkled brown kind that should have been a bronze bookend.

I usually made mudballs for Jim Teeman. He was the best thrower and besides, he paid the most. Whenever we made a good hit, we would say, "Amen, Brother!" Jim and I were Southern Baptists, but we decided to quit. They kinda have the right idea, but it all comes out wrong when they say it. Besides, it killed me when the preacher always faked a Southern accent for the sermon.

Well, anyway old Teeman decided I was going to put a rock inside his next mudball.

"What do you want……to kill somebody?"

"Aw, it'll be all right. It'll make me pitcher if they know it's me that threw it. They'll know a throwing arm when they feel that one."

"I don't know, Teeman. What if it flew down their throat or hit their nuts or something?"

"Jeez, I'm a better thrower than that. Look, I'll just aim at their hands and knock their mudball out of them and just let it hit their hands a little. Just so it's not wasted."

"Wellll, I don't know, Teeman." That was my stalling device that brought results.

"Look, Angie, I'll even give you a dime!"

Man, I hit the big time! I took it in my stride, though.

"Well, alright, but it seems like it'd be worth about fifteen cents if you ask me."

That damn fool gave me another nickel!

The white flag and I went looking for a rock. I found a bunch by the merry-go-round. I had to stop it and a lot of kids were pretty mad, but I told them there was a war on and gave them a push. You wouldn't think that would make up for a whip lash, but they thought it was fine.

I got hit with a mudball before I got to the fort and I was mad. There was no respect for the flag anymore! I was ready to throw the rocks alone, but I packed them for Teeman. I worked on the first one for about five minutes getting it round. Then my precocious fingers started flying on those packing jobs. Teeman was using up the ammo pretty fast. I thought that he would probably be put in the outfield; you couldn't trust him as a pitcher. He hit guys pretty close to where I was worried he would. Then he got a strike. He hit Billy John in the eye.

"Wow, Angie! Amen, Brother!"

I didn't Amen, Brother him back though. Something was wrong. Billy John kept holding his hand over his eye and standing there. Then he just plopped down in the line of fire and everything. I jumped up and ran to their fort.

"Hey, Billy John! You all right?"

He didn't say anything. I ran for Mrs. Cree, my teacher. Man, then there was an ambulance and everything, and Billy John went to the hospital. I swore I'd never touch earth with my hands again. That was a Friday and we got out of school a while after that.

On Saturday I didn't even practice baseball. I just sat around and sort of watched TV and read and cut stuff with the scissors that had turned on me.

I wanted to visit Billy John or at least find out where he was, but I was afraid. I think he knew who made those rock balls.

Monday at school Teeman was cheating off me in a test and our principal came to the room. He talked to our teacher and then looked us over. He asked to see all the people who "participated in the mudball fight." I got up pretty slowly. I'd rather have taken two tests than have to be yelled at by our principal, but I thought maybe he'd know what happened to Billy John. Old Teeman sat there for about two days and then got up too. We went to the principal's office. He closed the door and we all sat VERY quietly. I wanted to talk to Teeman, but it would have seemed like a sin or something. The principal looked us over like he did in our room, cleared his throat and began to speak. He didn't even yell. I wished he would have, though; it was really scary when he was quiet. He told us that mudball fights were very dangerous, but putting rocks inside was just disastrous. He told us that we were all to blame and then he gave us our punishment. It was a bunch of homework and staying after school junk. I thought he was going to let us go, but then he told us, quieter than before, that Billy John was blind where we hit him. I just about got sick. We all sat there for a minute. I decided to confess.

"I did it, Mr. Wells. I made the rockballs. And I threw them all too!" I was really in the confessing mood.

He just told me that we'd all be punished the same because we were equally to blame, and that it could have happened with a mudball without a rock.

The next night I went to the hospital to see Billy John. At first the receptionists weren't going to let me in; they didn't let anyone under fourteen through. But after I explained to them how the accident was my fault and all, I guess they relented a little. Besides, I sneaked through when they weren't looking. I was sort of afraid to see Billy John. I didn't know if he knew who threw the rocks or anything, but I thought that he probably guessed who had made them. When I pushed open the door, he was asleep. I just stood there staring at him. He had these bandages over about half his head and over his crummy eye, and he looked so neat and scary I wanted to MARRY him!

"Hi, Angie."

Boy, did he scare me.

"Hi, Billy John….here." I shoved his present at him. I wasn't going to give it to him right away. I had it all planned that we would have a nice little visit and I would tell him about school and stuff, and at the end give him the present and leave. I guess I was so nervous I just handed it to him. He ripped it open and took out his presents….a flashy cowboy shirt with fringe on the sleeves and front with sparkly stuff all over, and then this eye patch I made with sparkly stuff stuck to the glue I dumped on it. I'd wanted to keep that shirt for me, but I knew I'd give it to Billy John.

"Wow, Angie! This is a real neat shirt. Oh, Man, look at it under the light!"

He damn near blinded me waving that shirt under his bed lamp. He was going to put on his patch, but I told him to wait 'til he got his bandages off.

"Man, I bet you spent your mitt money and everything!"

"Aw, I didn't want to play anyway. I'd probably kill somebody the way I throw the bat."

I left the hospital then. We didn't talk about his eye. I thought I lied when I told him I didn't want to play on the team. After I thought about it though, I thought I'd rather see him wearing his new shirt and maybe he could even wear two shirts a week.

Duties

"This is an outrage! This I will not stand for! This is something up with which I will not put, as Churchill has punned! He shall be returned to school within the hour! Thank you for your call, Principal Stevens."

Hooky, indeed! I am the Mayor of this town. Does he wish to publically humiliate me?

There are three places he would likely be- my favorite places as a boy- but that's beside the point-he's my son, I'm the Mayor, an important person in this town. I'll thrash him until he knows the meaning of responsibility and duty.

The candy store was comfortably quiet, awaiting its prey-the school children leaving school at the proper hour, not like my son. After this, I shall never give him more than milk money, instead of telling him to try the licorice whips and mint drops that I enjoyed as a child.

Perhaps I'll wield the belt like my father used to do at times. He's never felt that before.

The pet store was raucous with parrots screeching for the thrill of hearing their voices, protesting their lack of freedom within the jungle trees and their formerly lush surroundings, as they swung upon their perches within the curved cages. They were as outraged as I just then. Dogs barked, hungry for lunch, while cats rubbed the bars of their cages, crying piteously for a chin rub. My boy was not by the ferret cage, looking and playing by the hour with an animal as curious and inquisitive as he, not knowing that Rikki Tikki, as he had named it, would be his for his birthday…..but after his hooky, maybe not.

Was it his day for the dentist? No, that was last month. Regular dental care, that's a must for my son. He might need two front teeth, though, by the time I'm done with his punishment!

There was only one last place to look. On the edge of the town was a park, a rolling, gently sloped series of hills with grass that was always too long, more like hay than the trimmed Kentucky Bluegrass of the city park. A little wild, like the nature of my son. There is a tree at the top, a spreading, climbable tree whose branches almost lift a person as if it wanted you there, with seating so comfortable and curved that it seems to say, "Look at what you have before you. Observe it, appreciate it, and have comfort as you rest from your obligations." It is the very tree where I climbed and gazed outward as a boy.......but only on Saturdays when my chores were done.

My guess was correct. Perched like a parrot freed from its bars sat my son. His back was to me, but his head was down, no doubt feeling some premonition of the guilt he knew he must feel.

I knew what I must do. I could still climb a tree; we had climbed it together in a race last year. He won, but not by far. We had gazed together over the rolling hills that gently sloped. His little dog Yappy waited patiently beneath while I pointed out landmarks and faraway places where we would someday hike. When we dropped from the tree, Yappy nipped his heels as he raced down the hill, leaping and racing behind him, nipping when he could, the joyful heels that were free from all responsibility for a day. My son fell and rolled in perfect log shape down the hill with Yappy leaping onto and off him until they stopped for lack of slope, then wrestled their way back up the hill toward me.

Today, though, he had gone too far. He had taken advantage of my good nature, and he would have to pay! How quietly could I climb, I wondered. What a surprise he would have when he looked into my face as I towered above him. I quietly stood at the base of the tree, removing suit coat and tie, and rolled up the sleeves of my clean, starched white shirt my wife had pressed the day before. I knew the shirt would suffer in the climb, but the look on my son's face would be worth it. I grabbed the first limb, which was always a long stretch. The rest was easy to a seasoned climber like myself. Hand over foot I climbed, hoisting myself to each successive branch, quietly, stealthily, relishing the look of surprise and shock he would have on his face, as he was caught in the act of his hookydom! Closer I came! He had to have heard me now, but still his head didn't turn to look at me. Was it guilt or fear? Both, I hoped. Maybe he wouldn't have to be punished if he appeared dutifully remorseful.

As I stepped to the last limb, I towered above him as planned. His back was still turned to me, head down. Was he sleeping, or had he fainted from fear of my reprisal?

"Hello, Daddy," he said without turning.

"You have humiliated me today," I returned.

"I'm sorry, Daddy, but I had to."

"You will have to be punished."

"I know."

"Look at me."

As he turned, there was a movement in his hands so that I could see what he held…a beautifully illustrated copy of Treasure Island, my copy as a boy.

"I could finish it today," he pleaded with his eyes.

It was my turn to show shock on my face. I had to grab the trunk to avoid a fall. I had to sit on the limb. It was the perfect shape for sitting.

Board meeting at 2:00, Mayor's office. He shall be returned to school within the hour.

"Read to me?" I asked.

Hunting with Jeremy, My Sister
......I Mean Brother

If I hadn't been born a girl, I wouldn't be stuck here reading this stupid book. I'd be hunting with Father and probably come home with more rabbits than Jeremy. I'd probably even get a possum. I think Jeremy would be better off in the kitchen with a chiffon apron around his pretty waist. He's such a sissy I can just see him jumping at the sound of Father's shotgun or sneaking behind him to hold his ears. If Father saw that, Jeremy would get a good cuff on those ears, fingers and all. It would probably drive his fingers clean up to his nose, and that would be about what he deserved. If a rabbit decided to hold still for Jeremy or come a little closer and paint a target between his eyes, Jeremy might be able to wound it a bit- in the side. If the rabbit has turned white for the winter, Jeremy won't be able to see it at all. He'd just aim at anything moving which could be Father or his own toe. If he's lucky, he might shoot a few berries out of a bush.

It's simply not my place to be out hunting, according to nearly everyone but Father. Once he did take me and I had been practicing on fence posts and small birds until I got to be a real dead-eye. I loved the sound of breaking glass with a shot, but glass was precious to us, especially canning jars. So anyway I was getting everything I aimed at- if not between the eyes, then right close to them; Father couldn't believe how accurate I was! I could see him glancing at Jeremy now and then with no particular look in his eyes, but just to see the look Jeremy had in his eyes which was a look of pure stupidity, of course, with some kind of fear, like he was scared of losing the place that everyone thought he belonged-out hunting with Father. I'll see about that.

Straight From Teen Magazine

It seemed only right that Mace should call me a bubble gummer the first time we met. The bubble that I had blown had become too large and thin to suck back into my mouth and it had exploded on my face. I might have been slightly embarrassed if I hadn't been so mad that I was seething. My face was a purple mask of Sour Grape. My seething made the film of gum over my left nostril form into a bubble that grew and shrunk with each breath and exhale.

I had been giving Mace the big eye for a while. It was when I was trying to make an impression that I really made an ass of myself. I thought he was a male model from The New Yorker, and here I was: a cartoon from Space Gremlin comic books.

Before I had a chance to pull out my gum and roll it around on my face to get the gum off, Mace was looking from his seat across the aisle and told me to pull out my gum and rub it across my face. I told him I knew what to do. He told me I probably knew what was new in the bubble gum world. I was rubbing the gum across my face slowly, trying to maintain some sort of composure, and the next thing I knew, Mace was sitting beside me. He grabbed the gum from me and started rubbing off three or four layers of skin. I was about half alive when the gum finally came off. He could have faded away into the sunset or the next bus stop, and I probably wouldn't have remembered anything.

He was laughing all the time he was rubbing, and he was still pretty damn amused when he was finished. I told him I didn't see the humor. I would have laughed myself to death though, if it had happened to someone else.

"Still in high school?" he asked.

I told him, No, that I was a mysterious woman from the Far East and didn't go to high school. He told me I was strange all right.

"I bet you're not a day over sixteen."

"I'm sixteen only in age, and my private tutor considers me a sophomore in college."

"That's certainly a coincidence because I'm a sophomore at the University and everyone considers me to have the highly intelligent brain of a senior."

"You have the head of a conceited senior for sure, and four people could join arms to try to surround your ego, but they couldn't begin to span it. I'm also very surprised that you go to the University, because I think you look more like a carry out boy at a supermarket."

"Yeah, I usually carry out everything I try."

It was his stop and he asked me when he would see me again. I gave him a description of my mother so that he would recognize her when he carried out her groceries.

"Then just jump in her car and come home with her, and there I'll be."

"I mean it. When can I see you again?"

I scribbled my phone number on a scrap of paper and told him to call me. I really didn't know how much I was looking forward to seeing him again until he left and I started thinking about him….a lot.

High school seemed really trivial after meeting Mace. I rushed home every day after school to wait for him to call. I was like the heroine of a Rosamund Du Jardin novel. When a week went by and he hadn't called, I decided it was time to get on that bus again.

I rode for about ten minutes before anything happened. Then, he just got on, pulling himself up two steps at a time with the bar at the front, his muscles defining an upper body in great shape. He sat two seats in front of and across from me. He didn't notice me until he was looking at a girl on the sidewalk.

"Hey, Bubblegummer!"

"Hey, Joe Pushcart."

He sat beside me and told me that he was going to call me, but he couldn't read the phone number. I was hoping he would have a good excuse. I wrote…..I PRINTED my phone number again. He asked me to go to a movie with him. He told me to meet him on a corner about four blocks from my house.

"That's different. Is that the way they do it at the big U?'

"Naw, I just don't like meeting parents, especially girls' parents."

I was about ten minutes late when I went to meet him. I planned it that way to get even with him for making me meet him on a corner, but I was never on time anyway. I thought my being late would make him happier to see me, but he hadn't even shown up yet! I had to wait ten long minutes for him. He didn't apologize. He didn't bother to walk fast. He had the kind of walk that would drive a bus driver to distraction…and girls too.

"Had to wash your apron?"

He told me he had to shop for a birthday present for his grandmother.

We went to a Disney flick-Jungle Book. I was surprised. I thought we would go to a sex saturated one with his trying to keep pace with the hero. He didn't try anything except when the python was slithering around Man Cub trying to squeeze him to death singing, "Trusssst in Me" and slobbering all over him, Mace slithered his arm around me and started kissing me, practically drooling right along with the python. I didn't know making out would be so……wet!

After the movie we were walking like the fat bear when he asked if I wanted to come up to his apartment. I told him I was no ORDINARY pick-up. He just said, "Trussst in Me."

He dropped the subject, though, when I said, "No."

He walked me about a block from my house and asked me if my parents waited up for me.

"They usually lurk in crucifixion position behind our rose trellis to blend in."

"No, really, they wait up for you?"

"My mother usually waits."

"You know how I feel about parents. I'll walk you a little farther and watch you. You'll be all right, won't you?"

"Oh sure, I haven't been mugged for six days."

"I'll watch."

"You're the only potential criminal I know."

I walked backwards and told him to tell me when I disappeared into the night. I was waving a Kleenex and being very dramatic.

He had asked me out for the next Friday night. I was glad Mother hadn't waited for me. I'd told her I was going to a football game at school with my best friend, Beth. I would have hated to come home happy and find out we'd lost by forty points. She would have had an attack if she had known I met a boy on a corner.

I had been experimenting with make-up to appear older. I ended up looking a little cakey, but definitely older. My mother told me I looked like a Madam. I asked her if she knew any. She didn't want me to leave the house looking like that. She wanted to keep me under her wing, but I usually got my way, mostly by pouting, begging and looking depressed. Then she would be miserable. She would practically drive me and dress me at the same time. She certainly wouldn't have done that if she knew about Mace.

I had been dating him for four weeks and I decided to tell him I loved him the next Friday night. That night I was about two hours early. I'd been getting ready all week. I was prepared to be at the corner for five or six hours waiting for Mace, but when I got there, he was waiting. He looked better than I'd ever seen him. I thought I should have spent more time that week getting ready. He reeked of aftershave. Actually, he didn't reek, but it was STRONG. My mother would have told him he smelled like a Madam. I really wish he would meet my mother. He smelled good, though. No cheap Mennen Skin Bracer for him.

I blurted out, "I love you and you smell good!"

He told me he didn't know I had such good taste. Then he said, "Yeah, I love you too."

We went to another movie. This time it was the sex movie I thought we would have seen the first date. In this one, Mace was trying to keep up with the hero. While we were making out, his breathing became heavier and faster. His hand gently squeezed my breast, and I pushed it away. He tried for the other one, and I told him I had to go to the bathroom, and stood up, squeezing between the seats, feeling a little dizzy and breathing harder myself.

When I returned, he ignored me for a few minutes, then the whole scene began again. At one point, he grabbed my hand and rubbed it against his penis which was hard! I thought he must really love me and be turned on by me! When I tried to pull my hand away, he pressed it harder to his erection. When I pulled my hand away again, he said, "Yeah, keep doing that!" I tried to slap him, but he caught my hand and pressed it down again to his penis. I jumped out of my seat and went back to the bathroom, staying there a long time until I recovered my senses and my breathing slowed down. When I returned, I sat four seats behind him. He got the hint. Some people need to have a movie theater fall on them.

After the show, we stood outside the theater and looked at all the preview pictures. We both seemed a little shy after our episodes and little battles inside. It took us a while to break the barriers we'd formed. It took a hippie chic who wasn't bad looking, but when she raised her arm to wave Good-bye to her friend, we saw a heavy, dark thatch of armpit hair. We both burst into startled and grossed out laughter. Neither of us had been to Europe! We seemed to have the same tastes when it came to ridiculing people. We guessed which ones had electric toothbrushes and which ones had no toothbrush. We analyzed which ones had the fastest metabolic rate, which ones had the dirtiest closets and which were voted least likely to succeed.

Mace asked me if I liked to drink. My friends and I had certainly taken advantage of my parents' parties, but I wasn't on my way to becoming an alcoholic like most of the people I knew. I told him I thought drinking was alright. He told me he had tasted a new drink and wanted me to try it.

His apartment was amazingly clean for a guy's. I had expected to find dirty underwear lying around like in my brother's room. He had a stereo with speakers in strategic points around the room. When there might have been a chance for my left ear to have a rest, there was another speaker blasting into it. I couldn't hear anything he said. I was always asking him, "What?"

Pretty soon it didn't matter to him if I could hear him or not. I thought I was being attacked by a rabid wolverine. It was worse than in the theater! I tried the bathroom excuse, but it didn't work, so I told him I wanted more to drink. While he was mixing my drink, the entire cavalry arrived in the form of his three roommates. I was relieved too soon. They were drunk and lumbered around, making complete asses of themselves, yelling loudly, calling each other "Fuckface" while pushing each other into the furniture. They finished my drink and made me a stronger one. Then they turned up the stereo a million decibels more. The stereo was loud and so were their mouths. Their wrestling matches weren't too unskilled, however, so I told them they should wrestle until they passed out. Then I almost did when they fell on me and made me crash my elbow onto the edge of a table. They told Mace I was an alright girl as I cringed in excruciating crazy bone pain.

"Aw, she's just a high schooler I picked up once."

They wallowed around and didn't notice that I was leaving. I walked slowly at first, thinking Mace would come out to beg me to come back, but he didn't even peek out the door. I ran all the way home, my choked sobs releasing hot tears I'd held back most of the night.

I would have gone out with him in an instant, if he had called me or met me on the corner, or something! But he didn't do ANYTHING! I would have told my friends who didn't even know him, but they would have said, "That's the way it goes," or "That's life."

It would have been hard to describe my feelings to my friends since I hadn't formed them into real thoughts yet. I felt a loss, but did I even have Mace to lose? Was I just a big nothing to him, nothing he'd had, so nothing to lose? Was I remembered in his mind as a childish high schooler with bubble gum still on my face with my virginity intact, just to lose him?

About a month later I thought I saw him from a distance walking with a girl, but he was wearing a hat, and I wasn't sure it was him. The girl was probably his age, maybe in college. What made me sure was that Mace teasingly fluffed up her hair and gave her backside a little squeeze. The girl just giggled, then looked up at him with a sweet smile that said, "You're my guy."

The Klepto, (Written in high school)

I can't ever remember when I haven't wanted to be rich at least for a day, to have everything I wanted and be utterly spoiled. So when I grow up, I want to be a professional shoplifter. To get into shape, I think I'll start training on my chosen profession immediately. I'll start with $5,000 Dolce & Gabbana outfits or full-length leather coats from Saks Fifth Avenue, little things like that. When I'm a little more skilled, I'll start lifting things like cars or yachts.

But when I'm much more skilled, and have become the professional lifter for which I'm destined, I'll steal a few larger things like islands or continents. No one will ever find out.

This won't bother my conscience in the least, for a few years ago I had an acute attack of conscientiousness and had it removed.

Dramatically Me and the Telephone Pole.

I was wandering to relieve the inner pain I had felt when my emotions of self-pity had tumbled down upon me, overflowing enough to give me the physical pain of a galloping gut-ache. I paused under a telephone pole, wishing I had brought a lunch, but knowing at the time, I had come out here to melodramatically starve myself out of existence to be found lying in a crucifixion position so that friends could mourn and tragically wail over my emaciated body. Now that I was somewhat less overcome by my overwhelming pity for myself, I began to look around, regaining my usual active appreciation for nature. As I was looking, I absently moved my hand over the telephone pole beside me. The warped, protruding layers crumbled beneath my touch and floated to the ground. I rubbed purposefully and heard the brittle cracking sound of bark-like strips. As the layers were removed, I could feel the greasy surface and watched the creosote oil slowly ooze as the sun tried its best to make the pole ignite and burn me alive beside it. (I wasn't quite over my mood.)

The pole looked taller as I stood directly beside it and placed my chin against the brownish-black surface. It was more crooked than it had seemed before. Its otherwise planed surface was marred by bulging cow-eye knotholes which added to my appreciation. I was glad to see that this straight-arrow of perfection had disclosed its secret of blemishes to me.

I could see the horizontal arms lumped with sparkling turquoise glass insulators (those valuable collectors' items), remembered my formerly desired death, and laughed out loud. My only answer was an alternating buzzing noise.

I felt the desire to climb the pole to look at the world below me, but it was all I could do to jump and touch the first foothold whose fiery metal would have sizzled my skin had I obtained a good hold. Apparently, it wasn't the day to die. I touched the pole one more time for a tactile keepsake and headed back toward home.

Skiing in Breckenridge

While riding up on the Falcon lift on Peak 10 in Breckenridge, I started chatting with the woman next to me who was from Bulgaria, living in Chicago. As the lift passed by The Burn, an expert run filled tightly with trees, she told me a story about skiing with her family there. As she skied with her four-year-old daughter, she stopped when she heard her daughter cry out for help. Though uninjured, her daughter was slightly inconvenienced since she had her helmet stuck between 2 trees! The mother skied to her rescue, freed the helmeted girl, then fell up to mid- thighs in the tree well by where her daughter had been stuck, floundering to escape. The Bulgarian woman rolled her eyes as she told of her daughter skiing easily to her father to report, "Mommy's stuck!"

The Gazebo

After we thinned some trees on a property in Crystal Lakes, we brought the wood home to a neighbor who promptly built a gazebo. We were invited over to initiate it by making S'mores, through his young grandson, Dominic, who rushed over, grabbed my hand and pulled me along, stating, "Hurry! There's no time to waste!"

The Horror of it All

The Table

She had always wondered about the table. Here was the budget antiquer's dream-the extremely solid, durable oak table with five sturdy, beautifully turned legs on brass casters. It had been reasonably priced, very reasonably, due to the fact that the top would always have to be covered with a cloth or extra wide runner or placemats in order to cover the large burn or blood spot which was so deep that it couldn't be removed without sanding a large divot into it. Others had tried futilely and had left a quarter inch depression after the bottles of Clorox had failed to bleach it, and the power sander had needed a long vacation. So she kept it covered with beautiful tablecloths and always had compliments about them as well as the table's legs, nearly forgetting about the mark until the tablecloths were changed.

One particularly busy month, the basket of ironing built up along with other guilt piles of "need to get to". The basket contained all of the tablecloths needed to hide the very noticeable defacing mark.

Though overwhelmingly busy, she still had time to notice the stain, every time she walked by it. In fact, there were times she caught herself wasting her valuable time by standing over it, feeling the quarter inch depression, and hating the marring effect to its overall beauty.

She began to spend more and more time at the table staring at it and having daydreams from which she would pull herself back to consciousness with depression and even fear. There was something there, something that she should know about the stain…needed to know.

The fifth day that she realized that she had wasted an irreplaceable half hour by staring at the mark, she knew that she needed to do something about the problem. She needed to do something about a lot of things, but somehow the need to know about the mark had juggled its way to the top of her priority list. She had also begun smoking mechanically again and would awaken from her fearful dreams, desperately smothering the burning cigarette on the stain.

Being a teacher, of course, many students would bother her, but Jayla Stevens had been bothering her with her father's requests that she return to the hypnotic sessions with which they had experimented. She had made the mistake of letting Mr. Stevens know of her interest in reincarnation and regression. He had come to school on a particularly tiring day, and had tested her ability to be hypnotized. He ended the brief test, feeling that she would be the perfect subject for his regression experiments.

She finally gave in to the Stevens' duo requests, since she felt she would eventually be totally crazy anyway with all the new obsessions she was beginning to entertain.

When she arrived at the Stevens', her request was that he help her stop smoking. If she could get the cigarette out of her hand, maybe somehow, the dreams would shorten, be kinder and eventually disappear.

She could tell that Mr. Stevens was disappointed. Curing smoking was such a trite topic, and regression seemed to be his obsession.

The session began with the usual methods, and Mr. Stevens assured her that her next cigarette would taste like smoldering dog hair. Then came the question to her in her hypnotic state:

"Is anything else bothering you?"

"Yes."

"Why?'

The hypnotist watched as her fingers begin to twitch as if trying to juggle a burning cigarette between them, and then rubbing it out on an imaginary surface in front of her.

"Are you still smoking?'

"I have to."

"Why?"

"To get it out."

"To get what out?'

"The mark."

"What mark?"

"In the…..On the….thing."

"What thing?"

"The table!"

"What is the mark?"

"I can't tell you!"

"Why?"

"I can't do this!"

"Try. Help me to help you."

"Bring me back! I want to live!"

"You are alive and well."

"No!"

"What's happening? Tell me!"

"It's Billy!"

"Who is Billy?"

"Neighbor. He's my neighbor."

"Where are you?"

"In my house. Stay away from Billy!"

"Who told you that?"

"Mother. And my daddy."

"When is this? How old are you?"

"Thirteen."

"What year?'

"1901."

The hypnotist's eyes widened with surprise and pleasure at his subject's unwilling cooperation.

"Why do you need to stay away from Billy?"

"He's ba…..d……very bad."

"How do you know?"

"Mother. Everybody."

"What does he do?"

"He's mean to things."

"What sort of things?"

"Animals. People. Small things. ME! ME!"

"Things that are smaller than he is?"

"Yes! I was smaller. I can't do this!"

"Try. Let's get some answers for you."

"I will die!"

"No, and you won't have these problems when we're finished. Keep trying. Help me to find your answers."

"Billy wants sugar! Don't answer the door!"

"He's at your door?"

"Yes! Don't give him any sugar! Run away!"

"Billy wants to borrow some sugar?"

"Yes He brought a cup. But he's lying! Run!"

"Did you run?"

"No. Mother always says give food away."

"If someone asks you for food, don't refuse them?"

"Yes."

"Where is Billy now?"

"At the door. It's locked."

"What season is it?"

"Summer."

"Is it a screen door?"

"Yes. Yes! Stay out, Billy! I'm trying to hurry! You can't come in!"

"Are you getting the sugar?"

"Yes! I dropped the lid! He's coming in! I'm throwing the lid at him! Help me!"

"When I snap my fingers, you will return to the present and remember none of this."

"Help me! It looks sharp!"

"Listen to me! I am snapping my fingers! You WILL wake up!"

"It's a knife, but it's dirty! It's bloody!"

"You won't remember any of this! Wake up! Call for your mother! Where's your father?"

"Billy, go home! I'll tell my daddy! Daddy!! There's the sugar. Go away! Don't touch me! Stay away from this table or I'll get you!"

"Where are you?"

"Behind the table. I'm going to push it at him!"

"Wake up!"

"I knocked him down with the table! I have to run! Don't touch me! Let me go! He pushed me onto the table!"

"Stop! No! My heart!"

The amateur hypnotist looked on helplessly in an agony of final understanding as her heart burst within her, draining its life's blood, much as her disembodied heart had done so many years before, on the table.

They Shoulda Recycled

Joe had heard stories about escaped criminals inhabiting the upper reaches of Federal forest land and had even made up a few himself, but they had never entered his mind much until now. Now, he'd welcome a friendly face, an unfriendly face, any face as long as it had a mind, since Nick's mind seemed to have left him. He'd felt a presence around him and had turned at the sound he thought he'd heard, but then passed if off as a sound of usual forest activity in this tree laden, vision limiting hunters' dream.

He and Nick had poached a little before in their seventeen years of hunting together, usually post season, when it was challenging to pack into the higher reaches to find the shy, frightened elk that had been hunted for a month. Their "careers" at this time of year lacked the spark that such adventurous he-men as themselves needed for fulfillment; thus, the risk of avoiding game wardens, diehard hikers and campers was what they needed to be invigorated- to be revitalized enough to last through the winter until the spring opened up the lakes for their other sport of fishing. The couple of trappers they had come across just grimaced knowingly, pretending not to see the illegal elk in quarters they carried or dragged back to their camp.

Where are they all now that I need them? Nick had been incoherent for hours, if he had even talked at all. Had it been hours, or a whole day, or two days they had been wandering, thinking they were moving in the right direction, ending up seeing nothing familiar, if they could see at all in this moonless, snow packed, godforsaken bunch of trees in the land they used to call the REAL Big Sky Country.

He turned at the heavy sound of a branch snapping and waited, holding his breath, without hearing it again.

It had all begun with a bet. Nick had bet him a hundred bucks that he had wounded the bull elk that had brazenly come close to their camp. Joe was sure Nick hadn't even grazed him, but he could never pass up a bet with Nick, though usually his bets were so stupid and ill-informed that he could hardly call them challenging. But he knew Nick would never let him rest with a bet or dare hanging over him, and Nick even usually paid up when he lost. They had been trailing the elk- tracking would have been too strong and skilled a word to use since rushing off at dusk, half-dressed, wasn't the opportune time to find tracks or blood- and....the storm had set in, they had become disoriented, and here they were, wherever here was.

True, Nick was far from intelligent, but Joe had always relied upon him and had even been a little amazed at his almost uncanny sense of direction. Nick had never needed a compass, and, if truth be told, he couldn't quite get the gist of one to orient himself. Nick had always been unfailing at winding them down, through and around game trails at dusk or in the failing light afterwards to their campsite and warm, friendly fire. How good that would feel right now. How necessary that would feel right now.

With exhaustion, Joe had finally just dropped his rifle sometime back; he had lost any grip in his frostbitten hands. Nick's had dropped long before. If they found the elk maybe he could somehow manipulate his knife, making one slit after he'd killed it somehow, and crawl inside to warm up. Yeah, right, the elk is following us, begging to die. He shook his snow-coated head to clear his thoughts.

What all had gone wrong this time, he wasn't sure of. They'd been in worse storms than this one before, maybe not as wet and heavy, though, and certainly not as long-lasting. This hunt had kind of turned into a four day drunk, but then, when hadn't they? When Joe tried to use the compass, he wished he had not relied on Nick so many times. He threw it down with disgust and confusion.

As they trudged along, Joe's first uneasiness began when Nick started babbling. Somehow it was different from a drunken tirade of unrelated topics. Memories he hadn't spoken of in years appeared from nowhere- his '57 Chevy from high school, his ex-wife (he'd been divorced thirteen years) the cookies he'd cut out with his grandma, for God's sake! He'd felt like hitting Nick, but he'd probably have killed him, and the thought of being alone up here or dragging out a dead body that wasn't a deer or elk made him a little queasy.

He couldn't hit his buddy, stupid and irritating as he was sometimes. As the saying went, you could cure ignorance, but you couldn't cure stupidity. Yeah, Nick was his buddy-his wild ass drinking buddy who shined in the woods and who was a real card when he had been guzzling whisky. He thought back to their campsite and the disorderly pile of Wild Turkey bottles that just might not get recycled! How long had they been up here? How many mornings had begun with two wake up calls- one by the trees and one with the Turkey? How many meals in all had they skipped in favor of that bird in a bottle? He felt almost as if he were beyond food now. He had the illogical fear that if he touched his gut, he'd feel a distended stomach like those skinny African kids in Somalia or wherever they were from.

Joe had never felt really cold before in his life. He and Nick practically owned stock in Cabela's, the outdoor and hunting gear store. They had insulated camouflage everything- tree bark camo, cattail camo, woodland camo, and all the gloves, liners, hats and undies to go with it. Too bad they had rushed off in their excitement of possibly wounding their first elk, leaving everything behind, to chase an elk that was no doubt feeling a lot better than they were right now.

The Wild Turkey had always set his fingers and toes tingling with warmth as he set out for his few hours of a hunt. Now they had gone beyond numb to dead feeling, and if he could see at all in front of him, he thought he'd see an inch or two of blackened tips. His insides felt that deep marrow-binding heaviness of wet chill that no amount of forest trudging could bring back to life.

His nervousness and anger had changed to fear when Nick quit talking altogether. He wouldn't answer any of his questions, even simple bodily comfort questions such as, "Are you freezing your ass off?"

Joe's fear bespoke itself physically as he grabbed Nick and shook him, as much out of desperation as the entwining apprehension he felt. He couldn't let the hopelessness that was taking hold find a niche that it could settle into. His shaking did nothing to lessen his fears, because as he shook, he felt the loose rag doll effect of Nick's helpless body give way to an internal shifting, as if something had slipped off of a tendon-like attachment.

He began to run, pulling Nick's limp-muscled body behind him, thrashing both their bodies against limbs and trunks in a mindless frenzy of urgency that fought against reason and direction. Nick's grunts were more those of forced expulsions of air from his bombardment by trees, rather than protests.

Joe stopped, having held onto enough sanity and decency to feel ashamed of himself and pity Nick, beyond the helplessness and fear he felt for himself and the situation. Stopping, he gulped large draughts of air which turned into sobs. Choking cries he couldn't control filled the air, casting an eerie, all-enveloping spell over his prison-like domain of bark-coated bars. He wrapped his arms around Nick, hugging him to his body seeking any spark of humanness. His sobbing subsided as Nick stared blankly ahead. Joe choked and hacked once, pressing his frozen fingertips to his face, trying to regain control over the terror that had surrounded and entered him.

The shuddering began. He knew that it was a good sign for a while before the helplessness of his advancing hypothermia took over terminally.

It was then that he saw the light. At first it didn't seem like a light-it just seemed…..less dark.

Joe stared uncomprehendingly and then suspiciously, protecting himself from the relinquishing of hope, if it were at last given back to him.

Walking toward the light, he forced his feet to a performance that he hoped could promise to result in new life for them. He thought he could smell the smoked sap aroma of well-preserved pitch-that woodman's much sought after, lightning zapped base that would burn all night and into the day.

Locking elbows with Nick, he half glided, half dragged, maneuvering him into the miniscule clearing that no one could have noticed, unless they were within fifteen yards in full daylight.

He wanted to throw himself and Nick onto the fire. He wanted to embrace it, burn his lips with it. He felt like consuming the glowing pine that sent tantalizing life-giving aromas to his blackened nose, the faster to spread the heat throughout his body.

"Hey Buddy! Look at this! Fire! Can you say 'Fire'? It's ours, all ours, and we're coming back from the dead! Can you hear me, Buddy? Talk to me, my man! We're home at last! Well, close enough. We'll take any fire we can get, right? How 'bout some Wild Turkey? Just kiddin', my main man! So, how ya doin', Buddy?"

Nick showed no reaction. He stared blankly ahead with no aware- ness of the new situation, not even attracted to the fire as even a contented camper's eyes are drawn into the light.

"Hey,..........Nick? So, guy, where do you think the owner of this little site is? I don't see a tent or nothing. Maybe it just appeared to be our one stroke of luck in this screwed up hunting trip."

It was strange to see a campfire not surrounded by gear, food or a wood supply. Joe's first sense of overwhelming relief was replaced by an eerie feeling of unwelcoming watchfulness.

Soundlessly, he appeared. The man was easily the largest human he had ever seen. Heavily bearded with hair in jumbled lengths that spilled over unbelievably broad shoulders holding some remaining threads of checkered wool, he seemed to be wearing skins of some sort- some hodgepodge arrangement of skins and furs that gave a gruesomely comical appearance.

Wisely, Joe didn't laugh. He needed to show this giant his grate- fulness, even if it included some groveling and hiding his extreme uneasiness.

"Me and my buddy are sure glad to see you! You and your fire are lifesavers I can tell you! I felt like we were going to die out there, and my buddy still isn't in very good shape yet. But I guess you can see that for yourself, can't you? You probably know like ten times as much as I do about the mountains up here, don't you? I mean as hidden as your camp is, you maybe live up here quite a bit of the year, right? So, hey, do you think you can maybe give me a hand with my buddy, Nick, here? I think we need to get his clothes off, what little he has, and could we get him in your bag and move it by the fire? That would sure help us out."

Joe was stopped by a look at the huge man's eyes. Lifeless as Nick's, it seemed that the fire didn't reflect off of them. Not unseeing eyes, they were more like…unreasoning eyes….UNREASONABLE eyes. Sort of like those of criminals you hear about who hole up in the mountains- the ones that grow to like it better than being with people. The ones with crimes they never have remorse for. The kind that wear little animal skins…maybe even human skins………..

Joe watched, drained of all heat he had absorbed, as the immense man "gave him a hand" with Nick. A tree branch of an arm reached out, lifting Nick by a grip around his throat, until his feet dangled and air danced to the firelight. Awkward fingertips on the other paddle-sized hand stretched forward and then almost delicately caressed underneath Nick's chin. Quietly and then increasing by octaves, there was a chalkboard scraping sound of facial skin ripping away from skull bone as his impossibly thick fingers were outlined within Nick's face, pressing ever upward toward gray matter in his brain. Nick's final reactions were animal wails that remained unanswered by any reciprocal cries of sympathy.

Joe, the Mighty Hunter, arms flailing, twisted away from Nick's helpless screams, emitting a shriek so inhuman he didn't realize that a sound so cowardly and panicked existed within him. He fell, continuing his hopeless escape, crawling like an excited toddler in almost comic desperation, trying to salvage the skin off his back.

Country Clubbing

Robert Fuchs was dissatisfied with his marriage. The demise had started with his taking the job of sound engineering at a large firm in Louisiana. He was a well-paid, inventive genius at his job, he had to admit, a little self-admiring. Since then, his wife, Marcine, had become entirely too Southern-too Suthren. She had joined all the proper entities-the Garden Club, the Country Club, the Donate-All-The-Rest-Of-Your-Time-to-Charity Club.

Where was the little Midwestern farmer's daughter he had married? Gone were the days when she would flash him a boob from her garden. Gone were the days when he would barbecue on the patio in his patterned boxers. She didn't even want him to cook in silk bikinis. What would the garden club think?

The problem was partially that they just had too much money. He made lots at his job, and she had inherited lots when the oil wells on her father's farm spouted out its 60 katrillion barrels a week for a few years.

"What is too much money?" one of the Bufords or Herefords at the club asked him one evening at a very proper dinner for 8.

"When it changes y'all and makes you something you're not." And then to lessen the blow and not sound quite so sarcastic and damning, he added, "Us all."

He had caught their looks as they glanced at each other, knowing it was all too true. The fakes, the snobs, the money hungry money makers who flaunted their dollars at the newcomers.

"Robert, it's time for us to leave," Marcine strongly suggested.

When she called him Robert, it used to be a pet name. Now it sounded so proper. They all called him Bob, but it came out Bawwb.

She had tried to change him in so many ways since they came here. She had him give up his black plastic, wide-rimmed glasses to switch to wire frames. She had told him he looked like a nerd. Why shouldn't he? It was an honest look. After all, his father had been a combination math teacher/band instructor. He had come by nerding naturally.

Then there were the $4,000 suits. What was wrong with those polyesters that never wore out? She was a snob and getting worse.

There were two possible solutions to end the problem: Divorce her- they would both have plenty of money. Or kill her and have her stuffed. She would be easy to manipulate. Then, as he would move her little arms and legs to the positions he wanted, she would take up the proper amount of space in the house!

But he still felt there was a slight remnant left of the woman he loved in that proper little Suthren body. Could there be another solution?

Their home was filled with the finest quality sounds a sound system engineer could demonstrate. Strains of Beethoven, Bach, Mozart, Chopin and the rest of the guys wafted through the elaborate speaker systems throughout each room in the house. He had jazz collections, rock, soul, blues, Reggae, even Hip-Hop. He knew his tweeters, his woofers, his cultured, manipulated noise. He could control sound so that Dvorak could hit the lowest bass or the highest treble and sound as if his violin section changed to vocals with the conductor himself singing soprano; could he use his skills to save his marriage, or would Marcine really have to be placed beside Trigger in the stuffed figures Hall of Fame?

Robert began to formulate his diabolical plan. He began to buy ribbons…the satin kind. He had blue, yellow and a vibrant red. He collected various pieces of women's jewelry. Babies' toys began to attract him. From time to time he would check his dresser drawers to find his old familiar objects of nerdism that helped him remember his happy past, and that spurred him on to retrieve it and salvage some of it from his deteriorating present.

Every corner of every room was monitored. He had bugs so elaborate and secretive that while Tchaikovsky was playing in one room, he could be recording Marcine's conversation n another. While she was relaxing in a specially formulated herbal bath listening to strains of Mozart, he could be straining to splice, eliminate and then save the incriminating evidence that might solve his marriage problem forever.

His plan would have to be initiated at the perfect time- a garden club meeting- the meeting of the most elite, the richest, the snobbiest biddies of the South. He had made up a flimsy excuse so that Marcine would be forced to have the meeting inside.

"The workmen will be coming to tear down the roof of the deck," he'd told her. There was a dangerous, gaping hole and the whole thing could collapse at any moment, killing all the high society in Baton Rouge in one fell swoop (one fallen swoop). She didn't even question him. The old Marcine wouldn't have bought that crap for a minute. She would have had to crawl up to take a look for herself.

The setting was ripe and the main characters began to assemble. The conversation was lightweight gossip, inane observations, unworldly, snobbish. Liquid systemic aphid killers was about as deep-rooted as the talk got. Petit fours, punch and coffee was the perfect time to pull it off.

As the ladies sat with delicate crystal plates balanced professionally on their laps with manicured polished nails laced through cup handles, the French horn section of a Mozart piece was loudly interrupted by Marcine's voice blasting through the four speakers that were well blended into the interior decorated décor.

Marcine jumped, rattling her cup against her saucer. Questioning smiles looked at her and then away to discover the source of the sound. Marcine's spliced and edited voice blasted out again.

"Those two are a couple of the biggest bitches in the entire garden club!" Eyes widened, then grew wary as they listened. Mouths dropped open unsophisticatedly.

"They can't even be original in shock," Robert thought as he lurked behind a door, waiting for the exact moment to make his long-to-be-remembered entrance.

Marcine's recorded voice continued. Robert felt almost guilty as he thought about how he had provoked the conversation after Marcine's very bad golf days.

"That Emmeline Danford and her slutty daughter, Eloise, can just kiss my ass and anybody else who thinks they can do any better than I can may also pucker up and lay one on my rosy red buns!"

All eyes turned in horror and curiosity to Emmeline and Eloise as the two socially acceptably slammed down their cups and plates (just enough to make a statement, not enough to break them.)

As they started to the den to retrieve purses containing credit cards with limits to infinity, Robert leaned his head into the doorway.

"Wait a minute, Ladies, I'm not finished yet."

The visible head had donned his old black, thick-rimmed plastic nerd glasses. Robert leaped into the room wearing a clown-sized red and black polka-dot bowtie on top of a 1960's large print snap front cowboy shirt. His rust-colored double knit polyester pants were held up by a wide white vinyl belt with a Harley Davidson buckle, completing the attire…almost.

Robert eyed the small crowd, enjoying observing their knees teetering the saucers.

"This is for you, Marcine, but dedicated to the Garden Club. I think I still might love you, so let's cut the bullshit."

With the click of a hand-held mechanism, Marcine's piped in voice over the amplified sphere was changed to hard hitting strip music. The ripping sound of Velcro was heard as Robert tore off the bottom of his pants at the shorts line to reveal dyed black hairy legs with black sox and garters above the motorcycle boots. He began to keep pace with the strip music side-stepping with a grapevine slide. Every 4th step was followed by a can-can kick. Then another sound accompanied the vibrant music: the snaps of the cowboy shirt were torn open to reveal the sparkling cellophane fringe of garish costume jewelry that was adhered to his nipples with adhesive, but looked as if he'd had a special piercing for the sordid affair. He shook and shimmied, nearly fringing Eloise Danford's face, who was systemically rooted to her chair; she'd have to be pruned out of it.

Robert sneaked a peak at Marcine. She looked as shocked as everyone else, but did he detect the slightest flicker of an evil smile upon her face… the old Marcine smile?

And then what everyone had braced themselves for- the Harley Davidson rider came off the "cycle"; the belt buckle was open.

The music snapped off leaving the only sound to be heard of Robert's zipper teasing its way open. Very subtly, background music filled in with "Dixie" as Robert played his zipper to the tune.

"Please feel free to jump in and hum a few bars, ladies," Robert graciously requested, which was followed by a few highly embarrassed titters.

And then, the finale- the last outer shell dropped to the floor, revealing the most obnoxious orange and magenta boxers that had a larger than life hole in front, but, who had time to look, because Robert, not missing a step, danced out of them! Shrieks and screams surround- sounded the room! Heads were turned away and eyes hidden as the real Robert Fuchs exposed himself! Tufts of hair were tied delicately with yellow satin ribbon.

"I won't take this off 'til my little trooper comes home," Robert crooned to Marcine.

His testicles were attractively bound in blue.

"I'll be blue 'til I have you again."

On his large member were a series of small baby rattles which he shook and jounced as castanets.

"Give me, gimmee, gimmee, the old Marcine!"

Robert gave a last kick, picked up the clothing scattered about, clicked the monitor and exited, leaving them with Mozart once again.

Silence abounded. Marcine inhaled, testing the flavor of the air, then sunk back into her chair. Then, in high-pitched squeals and bubbling laughter, came the responses:

"He's sooo funny!"

"What a doll boy!"

"Oooh, Baby!"

Emmeline and Eloise stood up, mustering as much huff and huffing as much muster as they could. Emmeline announced that the "Gazette will hear about this!"

Eloise announced shakily, "I think he's a- a-a-asshul!"

Their flounce was a little less pronounced as they had to retrieve their purses from the den. As they retreated, everyone gave them a, "Bye, y'all," followed by well imprinted Southern Belle waves.

Marcine sat, still dumbfounded, but her old devilish smile began to capture the curves of her lips.

"Perhaps I haven't been paying enough attention to him."

And then, from around the room:

"We thought he would never lighten up!"

"He used to be a little stuffy, but NOW….."

"Thank God the pretense has ended!"

"Is that what it takes to get rid of those bitches?"

Marcine poured champagne into the natural fruit punch and invited Robert to have a drink with her and the girls.

At the club that weekend the men accosted him.

"So, you're a dancer!"

"Showin' off for our women?"

"So the sound genius has some versatility!"

"Golf on Sunday."

"No fair using that new driver you showed the ladies!"

Marcine squeezed his hand. Then she reached under the table and gave a gentle squeeze.

Robert Fuchs was very satisfied with his marriage.

Nursing Home Beauty

The broad outline of this story was told to me by Brenda Leever whose husband, Robby, worked at our Cedar Brook Trout Farm in Broadwater, NE. She was a nurse working for a time at a nursing home in a small Nebraska town nearby. Relatives and a neighbor of the lovely woman gave the nursing facility bits of the story which had to be pieced together. I have filled in some details and embellished the rest.

That she had been very beautiful in her youth was quite believable. Her aquiline nose and her fine-boned look of almost selective breeding was still evident. That she had been very intelligent was arguable. Her listless staring and lack of reaction to any stimulus within the nursing home or without suggested autism on the lower spectrum, or advanced Alzheimer's . It took a number of years of working in the nursing facility before Brenda was allowed to know the story behind the stone-faced stare that reflected such psychological damage as to be irreversible.

It had taken much piecing together of relatives' sometimes accidental bits of information added to their intentional reporting for the files and records that allowed Brenda to fill in only a small part of the beautiful woman's story. The events that led up to her relatives' later discovery were partially fact, partially derived from clues that neighbors helped join together.

The woman had been well educated; not a rarity in those days, but an oddity in such a small town in Nebraska. She had likely had more than her share of men from which to choose, but she had settled on a large, dark-haired man, full of the electric vibrancy that bespoke confidence with the energy to succeed in his endeavors.

After her marriage, she moved with her new husband to a farm miles out of town and lost touch with her friends and relatives.

The woman and her husband were seldom seen, but on days that they had to come to town for groceries and supplies, she was withdrawn and seemingly shy rather than demonstrating the slightly aloof, confident demeanor she had worn before her marriage. Some people said that upon moving close to her while reaching for the same grocery item, she was seen to flinch involuntarily while raising her hand to a part of her face, either to protect herself or to shield it from sight. When they could safely risk a covert look, they saw yellowed blue bruises which had been heavily covered with pancake make-up.

A year and a half had gone by, and make-up on bruises and a slinking, hunched style of carrying herself seemed to be unwillingly accepted by the people in the area; in those days people thought that minding their business and not others' in these kinds of matters were best. It had then become evident that she was pregnant. Soon she wasn't seen in the small town anymore.

Finally, it was rumored that the woman and her husband had moved away from their farm. However, a neighbor happened to drive into the farm yard to look over the small acreage in view of making a purchase to add to his land. After pacing off the cornfield, he began to look inside the buildings that seemed deserted. He found one shed that, unusual for a small, trusting farming area, had a padlock on the door. Aimlessly, he pulled on the lock and thought he heard a sound coming from inside the shed. He listened more closely, but didn't hear it again until he rattled the lock. The whimper that emitted from the interior was high-pitched, fearful and human.

Frantically, the neighbor began to tug at the lock, unable to break the hold of the metal. Rushing to find a rock or a piece of metal to snap the padlock, he grabbed a broken, rusted shovel from the front of another dilapidated shed and began beating at the lock, each strike causing the whimpers to become full-fledged screams that gained strength in their terror that he was coming in rather than that he was trying to ease the notes of fear within the screams by entering the building.

When the lock finally released its hold, he rushed in and had to wait a few moments for his eyes to become adjusted to the dim light within.

What he saw made him forever wish that he had never had to witness the scene that lay in front of him. When he told the story to her relatives, great shuddering sobs shook his body. He never spoke of it again.

He had never observed such a look of terror, even in the faces and eyes of predators who ventured too close to his chicken house, to become caught in leg hold traps. The woman's endless screaming punctuated the malnourished condition that was so extreme that it could have only been stark terror and a keen, unwitting desire for self-preservation that lent enough energy to the screams to shake her emaciated body.

As he reached out a hand to comfort and aid her, he witnessed yet another change in her. He saw her curl into a fetal position so rigid and compact that it seemed she had shrunk in size.

Tentatively stroking her shoulder with his fingertips only, as one would begin to tame a fearful stray animal, he felt a viscous fluid that traveled the length of her body as far as he dared reach. Gently moving in closer to her, he found that he was stepping in the same thick, sticky substance and then, following a glistening trail, he found the sight of which he kept silent for a lifetime. A perfectly developed, full-term infant, alternately red and blue, was lying beside its mother, partially enveloped in the placental casing, its stick-like thumb stuck in its mouth. The umbilical cord, trailing raggedly, was still attached to the recently dead form.

The neighbor thought that he could remember carrying the woman like a tight, elongated ball outside of the shack and into the sunlight. He thought that he went for help rather than taking her with him; he wasn't sure why.

Eventually, her relatives claimed her and placed her in the nursing home where she remains today. Her husband's whereabouts was never traced to be taken to trial for beating and leaving his wife for dead and for the murder of his infant son.

The nursing home files, the woman's relatives and the neighbors could only tell a part of the story. Her eyes could tell the rest, if they would.

Some people are so excheatingly dishonest!

Living in Boulder
and Weld County

Quotes from
Caste: The Origins of our Discontents,
by Isabel Wilkerson

When others suffer, the collective human body is set back from the progression of our species.

Einstein, on prejudice: After escaping Nazi Germany a month before Hitler was appointed Chancellor, he was astonished that in the U.S. he had landed in yet another caste system, one with a different scapegoat caste and different methods, but with embedded hatreds that were not so unlike the one he had just fled.

The Atlantic wrote: "As Usual, Americans Must Go It Alone" regarding the direction during the pandemic.

The Guardian wrote: "To a watching world, the absence of a fair, affordable US healthcare system, the cut-throat contest between American states for scarce medical supplies, the disproportionate death toll among ethnic minorities , chaotic social distancing rules, and a lack of centralized coordination are reminiscent of a poor, developing country, not the most powerful, influential nation on earth."

American women are more likely to die during pregnancy and childbirth than women in other wealthy nations. With 14 deaths per 100,000 live births, the maternal mortality rate in America is nearly 3x the rate in Sweden.

Infant mortality in the U.S. is highest among the richest nations, 5.8 deaths per 1,000 live births, compared to an average of 3.6 per 1,000 live births for the richest countries, against 2 per 1,000 in Japan and Finland.

Marijuana and other Road Blocks

One of the places where Steve and I lived in Boulder was behind a trailer court. I could be polite and call it a "mobile home park "or "mobile manor" but for the fact that there were only one or two managers in the diverse array of managers throughout the years who were honest, smart, fair, efficient and actually sane, so "mobile home park" or" manor" would be entirely too euphemistic.

The sheriff showed up about once a week for the usual knifing, shooting, domestic abuse or drug deal gone bad. One unique event was the murder of a man by his roommate, complete with dismemberment. Police tape surrounded the trailer and yard for so long we assumed they were expecting the parts to grow back or reattach on their own. In spite of the negative weekly action by mainly transients and interlopers, the long-term residents actually had a sociable and even kindly camaraderie.

This was the period of time long before marijuana was legalized. One fine day as I cruised into the entry of the court, my eyes were soothingly accosted with the dark sage color on plants that were nearly as tall as I. There had been a raid on one of the trailers that was a grow station. The owners had stripped out anything that would block or limit the growth path and added pipelines above each room to ensure the lushness and vigor of the 600 or so plants that were sitting in the street within the park, seemingly free for the taking to some. Two deputies hesitatingly guarded the pricey merchandise, seeming to do battle within their own belief system that these weeds weren't so bad. Maybe they were uncomfortable with the clientele in that park, suspecting that some moved their quickest when acquiring drugs. Most of the plants seemed to be removed by the sheriff dept., but as Steve and I didn't partake, we soon went home, leaving some of the residents there to drool, connive and maybe take what they could get away with.

The surprise raid must have had a strong effect on one of the neighbors we lived behind. In the farthest part of our backyard was a double strip of evergreens that served as a visual and auditory barrier for us. I could see into others' yards, but they couldn't see easily into the yards of neighbors who lived beside them. The next morning I saw 3 large marijuana plants of "Randy's" who had placed them directly behind his trailer, so that only Steve or I could see them. They seemed to be of equal size as those plants so temptingly placed within reach of the residents during the raid, so I never knew if Randy had grown them and expected a raid and hid them in his back yard, or if he and one of his local comrades managed to make a deal with the inexperienced deputy guards. Steve rarely came into that part of the property, so Randy seemed to think his secret was safe with me.

A few days later Steve and I were preparing for a party that included volleyball. Steve was always an early riser, in so many ways, and was outside in the backyard before 7 on a Saturday, wielding his chainsaw to trim a few trees for a clear court. As Steve revved the saw, for practical and auditory pleasures, Randy rushed out of his trailer to our fence, red-faced and swearing words at Steve, some of which I thought I'd heard before.

"Goddamnit, ###%%@@@*****, it's 7 O'clock on a f......ing Satur day!!..........................Oh, hi, Peggy."

Deflated, he walked back to his trailer. The jagged leaves on fragrant plants were never seen by me again.

Peggy Goes to the Dentist and the Brew House

It was time for my appointment with the dentist to have my permanent crown installed. I had had to be careful with the temporary crown to avoid breaking it on a petrified onion ring like the one that broke the original tooth. I was promised an hour in The Chair, but was consoled by the plan of meeting friends afterwards at BJ's Brew House in Boulder.

How fondly I remembered BJ's when it first opened; the crowds packed in, wait staff practically sprinted in a friendly, excited way and the entire atmosphere was sending off sparks. During our first visit Steve and I ordered a pizza. When the "runner", not our waitress, brought it, he announced in a dour manner,

"Hun tusk." Steve and I looked at each other, hoping the other had understood. We had a number of animals, but none of them had tusks, nor had we ever hunted elephants or rhinos. Some of my ancestors probably were marauding Huns, but would have refused to be served on a platter.

Simultaneously, we blurted, "Whaat?"

With gritted teeth that ignited an eye roll, he slowly and with overemphasized enunciation reserved for morons, repeated,

"Hand tossed." We understood he was describing the pizza that he was thoughtful enough to deliver. He dropped it on the table, spun on his flat feet and slouched away, only to be remembered a week and a half later. I didn't have a chance to tell him that in the English language adjectives are usually followed by the noun they describe.

When our lively waitress appeared, we told her how weird the runner was.

"Oh, he's just mad because he was demoted. He used to be a waiter."

BJ's is in the 29 St Mall, facing 28th St, one of the busiest streets in Boulder, but safely set back from errant drivers sliding or being screechingly forced out of their lanes toward the brewery. A week and a half later, we read in the paper that someone had driven their car through the front windows. That certainly seemed to be no accident, but a dedicated effort! We were pretty sure we knew who the marauding Hun was.

My dental office was my selection with my insurance and proximity to my house when I retired. It always seemed as if the patients who were served there were below the poverty level. I wasn't really in that category; I was a teacher, so I balanced right at the poverty level. When I arrived on crown day, a young woman patient was there, either in severe pain from a broken tooth or in severe meth twitches. She leaped off the couch several times, went outside to smoke, or ask the receptionist if it was her turn yet. She left and went to the Taco Bell that was 4 doors away, brought back her food, sat on the couch while suspiciously and surreptitiously cutting her eyes at me with sidelong glances. Then she took her burrito and Coke into the bathroom with her!

I rarely had the same hygienist or assistant. They seemed to import a variety of them for training, and most were young with a variety of accents, so the diversity was always interesting. My dental assistant for the day was a young lady with few social skills and no sense of humor. Behind my back as I was trapped in the chair, she used her blower hose for 5 minutes.

"Are you vacuuming back there?" I asked. No answer.

When she was fitting my permanent crown, it seemed a struggle and I asked her if she felt like hammering it in. "I might break it," she replied, stating the obvious.

When she was taking an X-Ray, she jerked my chair to turn it towards the machine. Then when she was fitting my crown in, she commanded, "Breathe through your nose."

"Why, do I have bad breath?"

"You were steaming up my glasses."

I needed the comic relief that the clinic clown provided. I never found out his true role there. The last time I was there, he danced from cubicle to cubicle, teasing the assistants:

"Aren't you a little afraid, this being your first time and all?"

As told to his wife, "You know what dries up MY saliva? YOUR cooking."

When my hygienist for one visit was Chinese, she was always smiling and happy. I asked her if she thought I was being a good girl being so patient. She replied, "You're the Top Girl!"

On a recent visit my hygienist was a tiny, sparky Mexican girl who told me some of her fascinating history. Her father was born in Mexico to wealthy landowners. When he met her mother, she was a maid in another household. After two visits with her, her father decided to face the wrath of his parents and marry her. His father eventually forgave him and accepted his "lower class" daughter-in-law, but his mother never did. Nor would she accept that her granddaughter (my hygienist) was really a product of her son.

It was a school holiday, and my hygienist had no one to take care of her two boys, so she watched them when she could through glass which enclosed a room off the hallway. As she walked me toward the office to pay, I knocked on the window. The older boy ignored me completely, being absorbed in a flashing light game, but the younger son, who was autistic she told me, looked up briefly, avoiding eye contact, while displaying a thickly beautiful head of luxurious dark hair. He quickly looked away, but it was a memorable glance that bespoke some disinterest and a little sadness and lack of confidence.

It seemed that my crown needed to be sent back to be remade. My doctor, who was extremely intelligent and exacting, wasn't going to accept inferior work. He felt bad about my having to wait and then return, so I think he felt he was rewarding me by telling about an event that happened to him in junior high that he had "almost never told anyone." He had joined wrestling, and was grappling with a friend who had the reputation of being a juvenile delinquent, who told him to give him his candy bar while directing the pointed end of a nail clipper at him. My doctor was arrested for being an accomplice to a crime. I didn't really understand his story, and he always talks so fast that his thoughts are always a little ahead of his jumbled words, though amazingly, his hygienists always understood him. I nodded with pretended full understanding, so I could get out of there.

I left the office, a little exhausted, but was revived by a flight at BJ's Brewhouse that included a nice Hefeweizen. We had an exceptional waitress who didn't pout or insult us even once.

How Do You Know When Your Dad is Dying?

How do you know when your dad is dying?
Is it retroactive?
Should I have warned him in advance?
Should I have known when?

Emphysema: an extended four letter word.
What a complicated, vicious cycle it created.
Should I have warned him when he sneaked his first smoke at 12
behind the barn that's now 122 years old.
I didn't even know him then, though I would have loved to.

Should I have known when he disked the fields,
Maneuvering his tractor,
Swirling, clod-filled clouds of dust around his face,
Nearly hiding the happy glow of contentment,
As his radio blared
And he sang along?

Or when the wheat crop came in,
Complete with rubber fanned chaff that coated everything
Two layers deep.
Who would have thought it then to interrupt the dollar signs
That gleamed in golden kernels,
In the red Chevy truck with the hydraulic hoists-
The one he bought the year I was born.
Wasn't I right to reward him with his favorite Schnapps for each
anniversary of smokelessness?

I should have prepared myself for the day he and Mom visited us,
As the Boulder wind blew in the first bite of winter air,
While his breath gasped and whistled,
Forcing him inside.

Or the Jamestown ranch visit,
Out for a hike on a trail too easy for Steve and me,
But impossible for him.
At his shade of gray, we returned to Boulder,
Amidst too much silence in the truck.

No one but Mom could have prepared me for the day it hit too hard.
How I hated her lack of warning when they came to dinner;
He, pushing ahead of him the O2 tank,
Followed by tubes in his nose, clear, but never invisible.

How could they pass it off as a practical thing?
Speaking of mundane things, like weather and relatives,
Expecting me to reply as I peeled a potato to nothingness,
Choking back the layer of throat that had leaped up to burn;
Where only the stoic German in me
Allowed me to stay in the same room
And not to run to sob silently,
To return with red-rimmed eyes,
Ready to discuss wheat prices,
And how the farm was doing.

What quiet desperation my mother must have felt,
On the night she called me asking for help;
He refused to seek care.
Maybe a reaction to his Dr. Cah' scorn;
That he complained of too many ailments!

Too many ailments, with pills to match each one.
Eating away at him like miniature Pac-men,
To burn ulcerous holes.

"Tell him not to be stubborn," I told her.

The ambulance was quick to arrive.
"Breathing problems," key words that urged speed.

After the colostomy, he made a deal with the doctors;
To have it all put back together when everything was well.
He felt he had lost his manhood.

He never returned home.

Medication. What a euphemistic term.
The real word is Drugs, and the answer is "Just Say No."
Who gave them a right to steal his personality?
Is that when he died?

How many times did the need to breathe and the fear of not,
Cause him to snap at me
With some monstrous phase
Of a gentle man.

The nurse tried to cover for him and have him make amends.
But how to say, "Sorry."
When there's an ape inside, shaking bars, demanding release?

Our promptness to answer his demands were a test.
If we weren't quick, we weren't trying to help him.
My hand shook inside their protective rubber gloves;
Reacting to commands.

We had to protect ourselves from him!
Last indignity!
Or invite Greeley's noted staph infection.

Family made the decisions that could not be reversed.

We were called to witness his dying.
Why we went, I'll never know.
How can a mere monitor
Gauge a man's life
From full, down to zero?

The Inadvertent Christmas Story

I live with a half view of a land fill. I didn't choose that site; it chose me, and wants to continue to snuggle up closer and closer, hoping we can start becoming friends. Along with those unsavory lots come the garbage trucks. My 'hood has an agreement with the land fill people, to disallow trash trucks to sally down our road unless they had given us a pick-up visit that self- same day. Unbelievably, some of the trucks disobey that edict! When I have stopped drivers on the road, both garbage trucks and belly dump trucks to ask why they are using (abusing our road) their answer is invariably, "Because it's a straight shot from Brighton, (or Ft. Lupton or Wattenberg.)

With my complaints to the land fill, most trash trucks became compliant, most of the time. One company from Brighton, however, was determined to not travel the designated route. Their trucks were the noisiest, the most rattlely, the most defiant. I could hear them approaching a mile away as they shook the neighbors' houses near the road. Some days I would show the drivers the color of my nail polish on one of my fingers. My phone calls to the offending trash company did no good; the manager was always "on the road", some of the girls in the office would merely give lip service, never passing along my irate messages. I finally told one of the most defensive secretaries I would ask the land fill manager to disallow the trucks to dump there. She told me they NEVER would. I accepted that as a challenge, and relayed the message to the land fill manager. Suddenly, things became serious, and the garbage trucks began to obey, staying off our road until Tuesdays, trash day.

One day in summer, hot enough to melt the grease off leftover fries, the company's trash truck was leaving my 'hood when he broke down directly across from my house. The problem seemed irreparable, even though the driver pounded for a half hour with a ball-peen hammer, alternately smacking the back opening and swearing in Spanish. Half an hour later another truck appeared with a man who appeared to be the supervisor. He seemed to calm the driver, analyzing the problem as the driver periodically pounded. At the end of an hour, everyone had sweat pouring out of their pores, and I was rather hot too, just watching and listening. Feeling their discomfort, I asked them if they would like some ice water.

"Quiere agua con hielo?"

The supervisor answered in English, thanking me. The rider stated that he would like water, while the driver merely stopped momentarily to find a new spot to harass with his hammer. I poured water into 3 red Solo cups with ice, and left the pitcher which was returned.

The trash truck drivers stuck to their agreement, and only came onto our road once a week on the designated day. When I'm home I'm often outside checking out my trees' health, when one afternoon in December, 6 months after the breakdown, The stubborn company's truck was driving past my place toward the main road after legitimately picking up a neighbor's trash. The driver came to a complete stop when he saw me, rolled down his window, and, with a brilliantly kind smile, greeted me with, "Merry Chreestmas!"

I responded with, "Merry Christmas! Y Prospero Nuevo Ano!"

Now, I offer water to everyone I meet. It seems like a cheap and easy way to make a friend.

Building Theft and More of the Unusual

When Steve and I were newcomers to an established neighborhood, we heard some delightfully funny or unusual stories. A neighbor a few miles east of whom we would never meet, stole a building! He worked for a kindly Japanese farmer who ordered two steel buildings in parts to be bolted together. When the farmer became aware of the theft, he let the thief go ahead and keep it!

Plunging Through Ice

There was a neighbor who seemed to have trouble keeping our water rights straight, keeping more for herself when she was in charge. On a winter afternoon where we had had weather cold enough to keep a pond frozen, our neighbor, Jimmy, received a phone call from the "water rights neighbor" to ask if he would come over and help her and her dog out of the ice. The dog had fallen through, and she went in to save it. When neighbor Jimmy went over with a rope and an inner tube, he pulled them out. When he looked up at the house he saw the woman's mother-in-law watching the whole thing from the picture window! When I asked him if he had crawled into a sleeping bag with her to warm her up, he replied, "With the dog, maybe."

Riding in a Chinese Public Bus

My friend, Kathleen, was a world traveler. She wasn't afraid to travel alone into exotic places, while not spending exotic prices. On a trip to China, she did the unthinkable: she rode a public bus! With the chickens cackling and other farm animals protesting their lack of freedom, she, the only American onboard, found a seat while leaving a seat open beside her. A woman walked into the bus and sat between Kathleen and a man with a sack beside himself and her. Within moments the woman began to scream frantically and bat at the sack. People nearby became involved with trying to help remove the sack which seemed to be stuck to the woman as it thrashed wildly. Inside the sack was a large fresh fish with teeth that had become attached to the woman's rear end. Finally, with much frantic passenger involvement, the fish released its painful hold, the fish's purchaser rewrapped the sack, and the fish settled down.

Buffalo (Bison, most of the buffalo were
wastefully slaughtered)

In March, 2015, in Valentine, we were harrowing the pastures, breaking up all the frozen cow turds while we unwillingly dragged the stemmy remains of clover and blackened grass. Our property bordered the wildlife refuge. A few bison lumbered purposefully through the refuge pasture, kicking up black clouds. The next day they were as near to our boundary fence as they had ever been, only the whole gang seemed to have joined them. There were 60-70 bison grazing within 70 yards of us as we harrowed; it was like living in settlers' days!

Krabi, Thailand

While riding tuk tuks and other forms of taxis, we always asked our drivers' names. One was "Boy", one "Egg" and one was "Puss".

Such is Life

Zelda was a fine whippet. Even when she was a pup, her owners had the high hopes that were to be expected from such a long line of racers. When Zelda wasn't racing, she was practicing racing. Every day she chased the electric rabbit around the track. One day the electricity failed. She caught the rabbit and began to chew on it, but they only took it away from her.

Cutting Up Cowboy Boots

Steve, my husband, and I first met at a spring kegger in Sterling, CO. Beer was flowing abundantly from the spout, and many made it our goal to get drunk as a good college student should. He was dressed in a fashion manner that was outdated with a flannel shirt and black cowboy boots, as if he hadn't paid attention for a couple of years or had any fashion sense to begin with, but as I got to know him, the answer was that he just didn't care. I was with another guy, so he began to try to win me over…..by pulling out his pocket knife to start cutting his boots into sandals.

Our first date was in a "borrowed" pick-up (can you call something borrowed if you borrow it from the first borrower who forgot to remove the key?) We joyfully drove over residential dips at speeds high enough to flip us into the air, like riding a shock- less roller coaster. It was so romantic!

Some pretenders go to church,
chanting their hippocritic oaths.

Follies and Failures
of Craigslist

Robby and the Onesie

Almost July. Nearly time for the custom cutters to set up camp in my yard. These are harvesters who follow the grain crops as they ripen from Texas to Montana, even into Canada.

The crew boss with whom I deal is a rotund man who wears bib overalls that barely accommodate his ever growing belly. "Robby" rules his crew with a generous yet sarcastic manner at times that shows irritation for the crew's "lack of thinking".

The events that occurred one quiet Sunday last July made me feel both uncomfortable and a sense of repressed hilarity. I received a call about an equipment trailer I had on Craigslist. I was immediately uneasy since the caller wouldn't give me his location. When I insisted, he had to confer with a man who was with him and his GPS; I knew then there were at least two of them and that they weren't local.

My uneasiness was enough to ask "Robby" if sometime during their negotiations for the trailer he would somehow make his presence known.

When 3 men arrived I received a text, "We are here," though I was sitting in front of my house in obvious view. Without a greeting or even acknowledgement, the men exited their pick-up, leaving the doors open and motor running .They may have been from a culture that had little regard for women. The driver looked like an extremely powerful man who led the way to the trailer which they studied with an intensity that was almost eerie. As they did, the youngest of them continuously bounced the hitch lock in his hand and flipped the pigtail for the electrical hook-up.

The negotiations were that they wanted me to take off $200 because the "Rrussian" tractor they had just purchased was longer than my trailer, so they would have to add to it. My frustration must have shown because we all looked up at a sound close to Robby's trailer. He had come out of his camper and opened and slammed his pick-up door. Here's where cultural and differences of experience came into play. Robby stood with hands on hips with stubby legs at shoulder width. He wasn't wearing bib overalls, but instead, shorts and a top. What they observed was a stern fat man who would tolerate no nonsense. What I saw that caused bubbling hilarity to nearly rise to the surface, was a rotund tum-tum stuffed into beige jersey shorts with matching polo top—Robby was in a onesie! With his stance and hands on hips, he resembled a cranky toddler.

The 3 men looked back down at the trailer while I gained my teacher voice, "Ok, who's in charge? Who am I dealing with?" The older man rather meekly said, "Me."

I didn't sell the trailer that day, but felt my courage was revived by a tough looking child, barely out of infancy, whose clothing seemed to snap together, who led his charge of protection with his belly.

Follies and Failures of Craigslist with Mickey

The face leaped out at me and my head snapped back. It was a horrifying face, the substance of nightmares, with nodules protruding from his shaven skull. The slanted smile, bordering on the sinister, with 2 gaps where teeth should have been, transferred no kindness to his eyes which stared back at me, seeming to know I was shakily studying him. Not much scared me. After all, I had taught eighth graders. But this one got to me.

The face had appeared in Facebook under "People You May Know". How the hell would I know this apparition, and why? I began to read his profile: he had served in the Navy for a few years and had a lovely 3-year-old daughter which, according to his photos, he seemed to adore. His stated hobbies seemed normal, with nothing of the serial killer or Nazi taint about him. I had a nudge of memory and thought back to how I knew him.

The year before, I had just purchased a phone and sat on the bench inside Verizon after the techs had set it up. They usually like to walk you to the door to show their respect and consideration, but really it's so that you don't waste their time asking silly questions like: "Why didn't you transfer my contacts?" or " Did the Cloud absorb my photos and rain them down into somebody else's account?"

I was almost finished checking on Verizon's probable rushed negligence when my phone rang. In a frantic voice with a fairly strong Cajun accent, I heard random words: Chatfield, Kipling and axle. I couldn't piece together the mystery, and even if I could have, wondered what I had to do with the jumble, so I gathered all aspects of my high level intellect and asked, "Whut?"

I thought he had the wrong number, but he slowed down, spoke in a more Front Range accent and poured out his story. He had been boating on Chatfield Reservoir and as he drove away, his boat trailer had broken an axle and he was stranded, barely off the side of the road on Kipling, with traffic blasting by. He had called a friend to come and help, but couldn't wait any longer, so he wanted to come right away to buy one of the 2 axles I had listed on Craigslist. I told him I'd be home in 20 minutes, then texted Marie.

Marie and her husband were renting my upstairs apartment with the million dollar view of the mountains from the picture window, and the $59.95 view of my back yard. I told Marie in my text that she should come down in the next half hour to be amused by what promised to be an entertaining visit. When Mickey, the Craigslist customer showed up, he looked like a gangster that had grown up living that lifestyle. But with his engaging smile and relief to be about to solve his problem, he was charming. Besides, he called me "Miss Peggy" which always softens my heart.

I told him how he had to drive into my backyard to where the axles were. He had to avoid running over my irrigation hose and my Buffalo grass. He asked me to show him the obstacles. He backed his immaculate pick-up expertly to the axles, then, opening his meticulously organized tool box, pulled out the right sized wrench to separate the 2 sets of leaf springs.

Marie arrived at this time. I felt bad that she hadn't been in the apartment, but instead had been visiting her new grandchild, and her daughter-in-law had delivered her. She immediately came to the back, then Mickey's friend arrived. Gangsta!! I wondered if he and Mickey had been in the same gang for long! After Mickey had the 2 axles separated it was time to load them into the back of his pick-up. Marie, that tough lady, jumped right in to help. With the 2 guys lifting it high into the air, Marie lifted the lower part with leaf springs dangling dangerously above her head. She didn't notice or care; she liked to be active.

Mickey didn't have the full amount for which I had listed the axle, but told his friend to give him $20. Without hesitation, his friend opened his wallet and handed it over.

Mickey told us, "Thank you, Miss Peggy. Thank you, Miss Marie," in a very unscary manner. His friend nodded shyly and politely to us.

Later we heard the story from Mike, Marie's husband's, point of view. Marie hadn't let Mike know she had returned. Mike was watching the event from the window inside the apartment, horrified at his wife and his landlady practically being held hostage by 2 criminals, and forced to work!

" I didn't know WHAT to think! I had 911 punched into my phone and was ready to hit Send!""

The Continuing Follies and Fiascos of Craigslist with Wynd

I had listed on Craigslist the last trailer that Steve had built. It was a small one, very sturdy, of course, since Steve had welded it, but lacked a bed, so anyone who purchased it would have to know a welder or be one. I hadn't had many calls about this, but one seemed legitimate and persistent, although busy. I'll nickname him "Wynd". The first 2 times I returned his calls a secretary answered, "Wyndam and Associates". The third time, I asked her, "What is this business?" She told me it was a law firm.

Wynd made arrangements for a Wednesday evening pick up. First he had to pick up some baby chicks, then he would come by. He seemed a friendly type, almost jovial, and I had come down $100 on the price, and he asked for another $50 discount. Since he was a lawyer it didn't seem to be a matter of baby needing new shoes, but what if he and his wife wanted to buy a new Porsche? How selfish could I be not to add to the car pool?

That late afternoon my welder forgot to show up. He was extremely abashed when I called him, although it was understandable: he was young, 13 or 14, maybe 22, with a pregnant wife, and his aunt had just died. In addition, he was a ginger. He apologetically made arrangements to show the next evening. I waited an additional 45 minutes with gates open for Wynd to appear on our agreed time. Without a phone call or text, he just didn't show. I was very irritated that he had wasted my time. That's not uncommon with Craigslist, but I assumed a lawyer would show more conscientiousness. My attorney would have! He's responsible, philanthropic and a dear friend. Also, he's a Facebook friend, so I know he'll read this.

The next evening my welder showed up early. I needed him to torch a 2" bolt off a driveline brake we were dismantling. The first torch ran out of O2, the second one had already run out. We had to jump into the pickup, run to the neighbors to borrow a tank and take some time to let my welder gawk and drool over a classic car parked in the neighbors' yard.

When we returned, my welder got right to the job, torching a bright glow of heat to the stubborn bolt. The torch set-up was in front of a steel container and my pick-up was half way inside the gate- the gate that had to be accessed to remove the trailer I had on Craigslist. At that noisily inconvenient time, Wynd called. He asked if he could come and pick up the trailer in the next half hour. Without apology or sufficient explanation, he told me he just couldn't get it together last night to get here. I replied that he must have lost his phone and couldn't call. I told him that it would be ok to pick it up within a half hour but, "Just so you know, the price went back up." He sputtered a little with disbelief and said, "It went back up?" I told him that yes, it had.

"I think I'll pass," he said with a weak, wounded voice.

"I think I will too," I said with a payback kind of voice.

Without condescension and even with a little pity, he told me, "Take care, Peggy."

It was an appropriate way to end our dealings, and even fairly kind, so I resisted the urge to reply,

"Billable hours, Wynd, billable hours."

Dreaming

I was on the edge of sleep where the senses take on solidity-sound becomes plastic ribbons, twisting and weaving inside themselves and looping away. Where sight becomes an artist's perspective drawing with continuous action, following a thin filmstrip fenceline.

Traveling

Fifty-fifty

As my friend Kathleen and I first arrived in Greece, we walked along the sidewalk in Athens, dragging our suitcases, the obvious tourists, when a shopkeeper who was standing outside his shop spoke to us, seeming to practice his new found English.

"Hello, how are youu?"

"Fine, how are you?"

"Oh, feefty-feefty."

Sandhills Matron at the Gleaming Gas Station

As I traveled north, I stopped at a gas station in Thedford, NE. At the same time, an elderly woman drove up in a newish car with a custom license plate, unusual for that area; most sandhill residents seemed to like to get a return on their investments. She emerged from her car in a fluid motion without the incremental starts and stops from stiff joints, persistent nagging of old and new injuries or overstuffed parts, as can happen with aging and lack of exercise.

This was not yo' grandpa's gas station. It was of the new breed of truck stops/ fill-'em-up stations that was scrupulously clean with a deli and workers chopping vegetables and cooking food from scratch most of the day; it was fast food fine dining. The gift shop was alluring with its sheen. You could buy a bottle of wine or a purse sparkling with bling, and on a friendly day they wouldn't even ask for your ID or your gender.

The elderly lady and I were washing our hands, when I pretended to study her face before asking, "Are you Mrs. Olson?"

She looked at me with wonderment.

"Yes! How did you know that?"

"Your license plate."

"Ohh," she chuckled and gave me a light and playful backhand on my arm.

"Do you live here?" she asked.

"No, I live in Colorado, but I'm headed to Valentine."

She leaned in conspiratorially and asked, "Are you going to gamble?" (Rosebud Casino was 9 miles north of Valentine.)

"No, I don't really like to."

"Neither do I... unless I'm WINNING!" she blurted triumphantly.

Later, in the deli section she approached me confidentially. "When my husband died I got sick and couldn't walk. I thought I was going to die too. When I recovered I decided to spend my money instead of saving it. You should just spend your money while you're young."

"I'm not exactly young," I replied.

"But you're not 91!"

Seems like I had that same advice from some of my spendy friends. She was quite a remarkable lady, and looked far younger than 91.

The Rheumy-eyed Gallant Gentleman at the Gleaming Gas Station

Conveniently, or NOT, I was three minutes from Thedford, NE and the Gleaming Gas Station in the Sandhills, when my tire pressure light came on. I wasn't too worried as I had just had my car serviced at Nissan in Boulder, and they had ok'ed everything, including tires with that something/32nd stuff tread remaining that eluded my understanding, but I knew that was a pretty good rating.

I was familiar with the whereabouts of the air compressor hose. I had used it before on my journey south from Valentine, NE, so I pulled up to the garage and began checking the right side tires when a gallant gentleman and his friend drove up beside me. In his colorful, three years-into-outdated shirt and his worn, square-toed, but still in-style boots, this Don Quixote saw a Damsel in Distress, a Dulcinea, rather than an inconvenienced (not to be confused with incontinent) slightly irritated traveler.

The gentleman gently removed the tire gauge from my hand and asked how much air they needed.

"32, but I usually put in 35."

Pointing to my driver door, he said, "Look in the door and it will tell you."

It seemed those thick-lidded, red-rimmed eyes reflected a morning shot or two of "pain reliever," every day for life that perhaps slowed his reactions a bit! His hair was dyed bottle black, almost a shoe polish attempt, an unprofessional, maybe desperate attempt to recover some youthfulness he missed.

His friend said, "She wants 35. What kind of pop do you want?"

My gentleman Don Quixote paused to think deeply about the question, changing his mind twice, after painfully trying to remember the flavors of pop that existed.

With amazement, as he filled the front tire he watched the powerful compressor's pressure lift the car slightly, and knew he had to release the excess air, maybe quickly!

His friend and I talked about the devastating Halsey fire, very near to Thedford, that had devastated the man-made national forest, then jumped the highway.

When the kindly gentleman was finished filling my tires, he stood up from his one-kneed position.

"The only payment I require is a Christian hug."

I gave him a grateful, stoically unsinful hug and thanked him for his helpfulness.

Samos to Kusadasi

As always, on the third and last day of each venue in Greece, I was terribly, even worse than ever, hungover from my repeated introduction to ouzo which made me ouzzy on my ferry ride from the Greek island of Samos to the port city of Kusadasi, Turkey. I stayed by the side of the boat in the ready position to protect myself from well- deserved embarrassment and to protect the other passengers, whose faces appeared a little blurry as focusing necessitated more effort than I could possibly give.

What a time for the entertainment and honor of a pod of dolphins to accommodate us on the side of the ferry, leaping and diving in unison, playing and exposing themselves, not judging me for my over-imbibement, as we rocketed toward Turkey.

Juxtaposed to the honor of the showmanship (fishmanship/ mammalship) of the dolphins, my punishment intensified. As we arrived at the Kusadasi port, I saw that an immense passenger ship was docked there with the infamous name of Achille Lauro, the Greek ship where the PLF had boarded in 1985 to take over command and demand the release of 50 Palestinian prisoners from Israel, to which Israel didn't respond. This was the ship where they had shot and killed the Jewish man, Leon Klinghoffer, in his wheelchair, then threw him overboard, in front of his wife and other passengers.

Outside the entry of the customs building, taxi drivers awaited , frantically hailing us as potential passengers, crowding our entry, where inside, we were met (greeted would have been too forgiving for all our American sins and entitlements) by emerald green eyes in fierce Ottoman Empire faces, who checked our documents, then kept our passports! My friend Kathleen explained that they would return them, sometime during our visit. I wondered at what point they might feel like it, and would they kill us first?

Canada/Back East Trip

September 19, 2004

We began our trip in a huff; it took months to get ready, but Steve wanted loading to happen in ten minutes. We went to Frasier Meadows Manor in Boulder to say good-bye to Steve's mother Jean and her gentleman friend, Dick. Jean had forgotten to replace her film, so I handed over my camera. Two of Boulder's crankiest people glared at each other, and then glared into the camera, body language bespeaking the unspeakable (at least in front of Steve's mother.)

Gardening, trout farming, organizing and packing left less of our body fat to hinder our movements crawling into the truck, as well as not enough energy to stay mad for too long. It felt a relief to sit down.

Steve's ingenious invention of steel sidings on either side of the camper to hold our kayaks decided to challenge him; one kayak refused to be held in place. Steve tied it to the roof of the camper, then decided against it and finally wedged (rigged, jammed, forced, beat) the kayak where it needed to be. The 50 mph winds we encountered blasted at us from the south as we headed east. Our kayak could have been to South Dakota before we were. Our bicycles danced on the back bike rack.

The first stop was our "Potter place" in Valentine, NE, to view our lot possibilities for our new home, and to camp. Less cranky, we could appreciate the beauty of the place. The ravine on the west side of the second tier above the river gave us some protection from the wind. However, the middle section north of the little creek affords the best view of the chalky cliffs of the Niobrara. It could be beautiful in fall and winter, scorching in summer. Any home there would have to be complete with powerful air conditioning and a tireless furnace, since Valentine is a land of extremes.

On our way to Pierre, SD, to see Steve's brother and our nephew, we ran into road construction. Pierre was the only U.S. capitol that didn't have an interstate highway directly to it, but it seemed they were plugging away at it. The high winds continued. An eighteen-year-old boy was risking his face holding up a stop sign, blocking it with his forearm. Maybe he'd been hit a time or two with the sign. His two front teeth were ground down by construction signs, tobacco or abusive parents; he looked as if he'd had a hard life. As we questioned him, he answered in monosyllables, seeming to look straight ahead while a wandering eye eerily kept track of us, as if he suspected we would leap out and steal his sign, putting him out of work.

As we left the sign boy, we came upon the construction crew wearing white scarves around their faces to protect themselves from the asphalt bits that flew at them with high velocity.

"What do you think of South Dakota so far?" I asked Steve.

Second stop-Steve's brother's office in Pierre, SD. We stopped for a break at a park by the Bad River. Is it so bad to be a mud hole? Bad River Days, a Cheyenne celebration, were beginning to happen in Ft. Pierre, the "bad side of town." We crossed the Missouri River to enter Pierre from Ft. Pierre.

Our nephew gave us a tour of the park by the Oahe Dam of the Missouri River where he drives a ski boat for his friends, for fishing and hunting. During hunting season, we were told there might be as many as 500 wounded geese on the frozen lake which draws hundreds of eagles.

We stayed Tuesday night in Minnesota at Myre/Grand Island State Park. The oak trees were much like Valentine's with hiking and biking trails meandering not far from our site. We heard from our suspicious camp hostess (we were going to pay for our site sometime) that we had missed out on 12" of rain last week.

We moved our camper through Minnesota on I-90 to SH 16 to SH 52. What eye candy to see the tidy farms with acres of mowed lawns and freshly painted homes. Slender, domed silos rose into the sky like shining dildos. We took pictures of these while on the move, and our truck mirror is a beautiful accessory in many of them.

We stayed near Ottawa and Joliet at Starved Rock State Park. We had no time to explore what looked like beautiful hikes. A brochure explained the history of the name; Chief Pontiac of the Ottawa tribe was killed by Illinois-Peoria braves after attending a tribal gathering. For pay backs, Potawatomie and Ottawa Indians held Illinois on top of a 125' limestone rock until they starved to death. Eww!

We chose the largest campsite at the end of the park to give our dog, Ike, a little space, and so that we could surreptitiously drink a beer. Our volunteer ranger seemed to want to be our friend and maybe had no sense of smell or no sense of why we stood so far from him to talk and exhale. He proudly told us that we had chosen a good site because Bob Unser had stayed at our campsite since it was big enough for his million dollar car and trailer.

Chicago traffic was held up for 20 minutes for a 30 cent toll! I threw in 35 cents. I should have waited 20 more minutes for 5 cents change. Then, Chicago's and my foresight would have matched.

On to Michigan. We wanted to picnic in Stevensville at Grand Mere State Park on Lake Michigan, but since we couldn't find it immediately, Steve chose a grassy area by a bowling alley to set up our stove. Some people lunch on the bank of Lake Michigan; we chose high class bowling alleys.

Our friends, Chris and Carla's place on ten acres showed back-breaking work. Since I had seen it probably 10 years before, they had added another deck, an arbor, a fire ring, a few thousand perennials, and the beginning of an orchard to commemorate Carla's father. The artist in Carla was displayed beautifully.

Steve had never seen their place, so we had traveled under Lake Michigan, adding another 1,000 miles.

To travel into Canada, we had to travel over Mackinac Bridge. They had a radio station to tune into for the bridge report. It spoke warnings of high winds. Carla told about a girl who in summer drove her compact car over the bridge in a high wind, lost control, went into the river and drowned after a break-up with her boyfriend.

We hit it on the weekend, and there were hordes of hunters going into the Upper Peninsula.

Near Mackinac Bridge, we ran into a little UP humor. Playing at a hotel/motel was "Guys on Ice, an Ice-Fishing Musical".

At Lake Superior Provincial Park, Chris and Carla's favorite park, we stayed at Agawa Bay Campground. At the high-tech visitor center they had push button videos. One of the sign- in logs was for recording animal sightings. Some people reported chipmunks, rabbits, moose, but one broke out of the mundane by signing in with a report of having seen Sasquatch, sighted at a Wawa truck stop. (A town north of the park.)

We camped on the beach and had a picnic table by one of the few trees that hadn't been cut down for firewood. There's nothing like freezing lake breezes to make one sleep well.

The first day we hiked Orphan Lake, a 6 mile hike packed with ferns, steep natural rock stairs with roots crowning the trail. The strange name came from two trapper brothers who felt like orphans when they had to remain overnight during winter. Waah! I wonder how the animals felt that had to stay overnight with their legs in a trap.

We kayaked the next day on Kenny Lake. It must have been appropriate for "shorter kayaks," Chris's whispered embarrassment to a ranger regarding our amateurish versions of his and Carla's sleek ones, the obvious more professional models. The lake was right beside Hwy 17, too noisy for real enjoyment, so we portaged 200 yards to Lake McGregor, or was it 200 miles? The exit was marked by little yellow portage signs. When we had arrived at the lake, Carla was speaking loudly to Chris because she couldn't find her camera. A couple on the mound of an island in the lake got up and left. Too bad we didn't catch then at something. We kayaked by 3 beaver huts. We couldn't hear noises inside as we could at some others. I could feel heat radiating off the rock wall on the lake.

The last day at Superior Provincial Park we walked some of the Coastal Trail from the closed campsites, which involved climbing boulders and walking the beach.

We visited Agawa pictographs the Aswagos made 1100 years ago. Made of red ochre, oil and animal fat, they had survived all those eons: Chris said he couldn't even keep paint on his deck!

There were lots of danger signs which said that people had died on the rocks. Water was crashing against the cliff where people could get a close-up of the pictographs. There were chains, ropes, a life buoy and a long hook nearby. Steve walked it boldly. On the way out we walked between two narrow cliffs which looked like they had been a secret passageway.

Chris and Carla had to return home for work: I could feel her envy that I had retired and that I wasn't going to work on Monday.

We decided to travel farther north into Canada before traveling east again. We moved onto Timmins where Steve popped in a Shania Twain CD. As I looked up the town in our AAA book, it said Shania had been raised in Timmins. We traveled in driving rain and stayed at a boat ramp at Dana Jowsey Lakes Provincial Park. We could hear pounding rain and loons all night.

We stopped to look at Kettle Lakes Provincial Park, at which we will camp for a week if we ever return to Canada. There were beautiful bike roads-ones where a dog could run and bountiful lakes for swimming. We liked their liability disclaimer: "No lifeguard on duty. Parents, children are your responsibility," A ranger said, "That takes care of our responsibility." We thought about the multiple lawsuits that are filed in the U.S. We regretfully decided to move on to travel in the rain, although this would have been the best spot to stay.

Sept. 28-30. We found the gate open to Marten River Provincial Park which was closed, but open. They had left it open for their seasonals-people who live there for months at a time. No one checked up on us. For two days we had the tent area to ourselves. We took beautiful hikes by 200 and 300 year old white fir trees, prized for their straight growth. The area had been inaccessible, so the English had to forego cutting their masts from these trees. We learned that sphagnum moss was used for absorbent bandages by Indians.

We kayaked the Marten Bay and River where we stopped to visit an old logging camp complete with interpretive signs. Huge square logs from former days were on the ground containing 352 board feet within.

We met two seasonals, P and G from Ontario, former alcoholics they told us, who wanted to talk. Apparently we 4 made up 6 people in all of the park. We saw campers parked for the duration with a $1000 or $900 fees attached.

P, our new friend, told of mental patients from North Bay who were brought out for a day and seemed calmer by the end of the day. She thought that a handicapped fisherman there who had had a house fall on him walked better after a few days at Marten River. Her husband, G, was balding, and P said that she had rubbed natural herbs, sage and others as she recalled, onto G's bald head and he sprouted new growth. P. was a gentle soul who liked colors. She had turned down a grocery store job where she would have had to wear black and white clothes because the $10/hour wasn't worth it if it meant she had to give up her colors.

While kakyaking under the bridge, I talked to an older Ontarian who was strolling on top. He observed, "The water's like a mirror, eh?"

10/1 Pembroke, Canada. While packing groceries we were "accosted" by a man about 60ish who looked concerned.

"Are you two ok? Do you need help?" Steve told him we were looking for a campground. He closed his eyes and thought for so long I thought we had run into Forest Gump. He smelled bad and had his top pants button undone. He finally came up with three suggestions, all of which turned out to be correct locations. Steve asked if I was writing down his directions. I told him I was just listening, although I'd stopped long ago. He gave suggestions about the cheapest places to buy meat, veggies and household items. Steve was very decent to him; I wasn't. He ended with: "I've traveled and been in strange places before, so I know how it is."

I was ashamed of myself.

When we found Riverside Park, it was exactly where he said it would be. It was a decent deal where it had a well-used bike and walking trail on the Ottawa River. A new beautiful retirement home was under construction. Canada takes care of its elderly. Why not, with a 15% tax? A tweed-coated man on the path told me the U.S.

had looked into their health care plan, but it might not be the ideal to follow.,

The Race for the Cure, breast cancer group dressed in pink sweats, pink rollers and pink accessories, were decorating the trail with pink pinwheels, but it poured rain the day of the race. They seemed to sit in a booth with no customers.

We were given a tip by some fellow campers that Bonnechere Provincial Park was beautiful, so we added it to our itinerary.

Bonnechere's lovely water sites were closed, but we stayed at an ethereally beautiful campsite, where white pine trees had shed needles for years, making soft walking and reflecting sunlight so that it seemed bright even on cloudy days. Unfortunately, we camped by a rowdy, undisciplined toddler who disturbed the slide show a naturalist narrated at the visitor center. Mike, the naturalist, began with the premise that naturalists wanted to gather research in the Bonnechere area on the gray wolf; instead, the DNA gathered showed that they were studying red wolves which had remained only in areas around Florida and the Bonnechere Valley area above the Great Lakes in Canada. Coincidentally, I had been reading about red wolves in the book, Prodigal Summer, by Barbara Kingsolver.

Mike said that as he watched the wolf pups one afternoon, they suddenly slunk down through the grass and out of sight; a black bear had arrived around their area.

One of the locals who had come to the slide show/lecture asked a question following up on Mike's statement that the Alpha male and female were the only ones who mated and had a litter of pups, unless more pups were needed in a pack. The question was: "What if other wolves in the pack decide that it's a good idea to mate as well?"

Mike replied that the Alpha male would physically stop them.

Steve whispered, "Sammy!" to me. Sammy was our neutered barn cat whose half-sister Buffy was mating with her son, LeRoy, outside the barn door. All the other cats were there, casually enjoying the sun. When Buffy began to yowl, Sammy leaped up, threw a cross body block on LeRoy, sending him into the barn. The remaining cats and Sammy went back to calmly sunbathing.

After the question and answer period, and after the naturalist had to ask for the noise in the audience to be stopped: our neighbor loudmouthed toddler, talking and scooting a squealing chair across the floor/clueless mother, we went to a "Howling". About 30 cars drove into Algonquin Provincial Park, the most immense park in Ontario. Mike's rules were simple:

1. Back cars in.
2. Shut doors quietly.
3. Walk and talk quietly.

The reality and response of the forgetful or neglectful:

1. Car doors slammed.
2. Horns honked as they were electronically locked.

When we were gathered, Mike had us look at star formations, and told us to cup our ears in the direction of howls if we heard them. He told us that his August howling had been unsuccessful.

After a slight, dramatic pause, he howled a long, mournful wail with a very noticeable tone drop at the end. Nobody home; no reply. He waited and howled more varied notes. After a long wait, he tried a very insistent bark/howl. After no response, he said sometimes they respond to group howls, so we were to have 5-6 of us howl. After a dozen of us howled with no response, he began talking. Some locals behind me told him to shush. In the very far distance we could just barely discern a pack howling. After Mike again howled the insistent call with no response, he hooted barn owl calls and received two replies.

We all returned to our cars and drove on to another spot by a lake surrounded by hills, still in Algonquin Provincial Park. Mike's same rules applied and because people had felt embarrassed and had learned their lesson the first time they had parked and honk locked their cars, only 3 of them did it again!

Mike wasted no time sending out his 3 howl styles. Instantly after the last howl, directly above us on one of the hills, Mike's howls were returned with an entire pack's howls, including puppy yaps. When he howled again, the reply was a single leader call that Mike said also told the pups to be quiet. He said that this was the first time he had had two different responses during a howling. He said that was all for the evening. He didn't like to "keep after a pack."

When we returned to our truck, Steve said that he thought for sure that he had heard our dog, Ike, howling along with the wolves, from the truck.

It would have been hard to top that evening in a campground, so it was time to move on. The name "Thousand Islands" had intrigued me from the second I had seen its name in our AAA handbook. To have so many islands, and then to dot them with mansions seemed to merit a visit. The last Canadian town we would visit and cruise from was Gananoque (Ga non awk way).

The most immense and spread out estate was Boldt Castle. The story behind it was both sad and fascinating. The proprietor of the Waldorf-Astoria built the granite, turreted castle for his wife, who died. The entire estate sat empty for 75 years, then was restored, along with antique boats on display in the boat house.

Other famous people's homes included Kate Smith's as well as Irving Berlin's house called "Always" (composed there). We saw the shortest bridge between the U.S. and Canada, privately owned, twenty yards long.

Some islands were built up on rock with dirt added to the rocks. One had no pretense. It was called "Artificial Island".

After being turned down twice at motels because they didn't accept dogs, once by a witchy old hag whose untamed, ungroomed hair looked far less domesticated than Ike's and whose motel had listed in the AAA book that they did indeed take dogs, we found a reasonable owner of a Ramada Inn. It was said that he was partial to dogs. Most motels that accept dogs seem to want them pock-et-sized, but he thought that it was the small dogs that tore up things in the rooms.

Ike was popular at the Ramada with nearly everyone saying, "Beautiful dog," and stopping to pet her. She was equally admired and petted at Acadia National Park in Maine.

When we had first entered Canada, we had all our papers in order for Ike with the help of our veterinarian and Steve's brother, and we expected to have to answer a few questions about her and have some delays. The border guard was probably in his late twenties or very early thirties. He tried to be officious.

"Sir, what do you do for a living?"

"I raise trout."

"And what does your wife do?"

"She's a retired teacher."

"And, uh, doyouhaveanyfishintherenow?'

When we burst into laughter at the thought of fish swimming around in our camper, filled with water, I think the guard felt a little embarrassed and left out of the private joke. To cover his lack of understanding, he stated, "You may go through."

When we crossed the border back into the U.S. with much the same ease, with my teasing Steve about his first passport in front of the young border guard lady, she good-naturedly told me that I needed to sign my passport.

Very close to the interstate we came upon Bolton Landing, Lake George, upstate New York. After 17 years of their absence from Boulder, we were going to get to visit J. and N.! In their area of Lake George, (Bolton Landing) their water still passed inspection to be able to drink straight from the lake. N. seemed extra glad to see us. I was relieved and happy; she seemed to be able to take us or leave us, usually. She and her mother owned and ran a book and gift shop. N. had a book signing that night at the store with the author there. He and other guests invited her to go for a drink at the bar nearby. She told them that she couldn't join, then joined us there while they sat at the bar. She tried to stay a little hidden from them, but that was difficult in a small burg. She was nearly as embarrassed then as when we visited a small shop in town. I tried on various lotions, and then when we left the last shop, I wanted her to smell an extra delicious scent, so I told her to smell as I held my fingers in front of her nose. Across the street were local guys repairing the pavement who watched. She may have been embarrassed, but I knew I'd never see those fellow again.

Inside J. and N.'s hundred-year-old house, J. had remodeled their kitchen and installed cherry cabinets, which added warmth to the interior. Their island had a range and kitchen bar.

We took a cocktail cruise in their boat which involved driving 5 minutes to N.'s parents' boat dock, and taking the boat out on Lake George.

The next day we took their boat to the state boat dock and hiked Black Mountain-a 1500 feet rise. It had had some heavy rains in the summer and looked steep, rocky and exposed. It was a painful hike with my plantar fasciitis, but had beautiful, colorful views at the top of the Adirondacks and Lake George.

N.'s sister K. invited us to have a cocktail or lunch cruise on the St. Louis, a boat built in 1896 with beautifully finished wood and director chairs. With a cruising electric motor, we could barely hear it start. The 10 mph speed meant that the power would last for hours, but any faster would suck the energy.

The Bixby estate is in the Bolton Landing book of the rich and famous of which H., K.'s husband is a part. It's a colonial estate with a colonial boat house to match. The inside has a common family room and lobby, and is divided into apartments. K. and H. have #2. The extended Bixby family consists of 200 people.

J. and N. took us to Clay Island where N.'s family has a "camp" including a beautiful house/cabin J. built which almost touches Lake John. About 6' of rocks separate it from the lake. They have to move inland when winter comes with its ice freezes. The huge sliding doors were German made and could work in combination to be all open or anything in between. There is a "cocktail deck" almost touching the water. In the back were the boat dock and sunning decks. There were 2 more cabins. Inside, each of the bunk beds had separate windows for looking out.

Back at J. and N.'s house, they had ancient hydrangea bushes in full bloom. Since it was going to freeze, we covered them with sheets, and the next day picked many of them and posed for pictures. N. was going to dry them and sell them at her store. J. just wanted to rip out both bushes.

N. bought a cake for my birthday, complete with candles! She told us to come by on our way back from our trip and we'd kayak Lake George.

Clever signs during the trip demonstrated people's ability to laugh at themselves:

In Milbridge, Maine: "Drop Anchor Realty"

In Farmington, Maine: an election sign: "We're for Kerry.... all 11 of us."

In Farmington, Maine: "We're proud of our state, ayuh!"

In Harrington, Maine: a "junque" shop named "Redemption"

In Cooperstown, NY, in Glimmerglass State Park, a restroom stall door's brand name: "Hiney Hiders"

We joined the millions of other Leaf Peepers in Maine who went to Acadia National Park and Bar Harbor (Bah Habuh) on Columbus Day weekend. Shuah we did.

Columbus Day weekend, 10/9-10/11, coincided with Canadian Thanksgiving. We saw cars from Quebec and heard French spoken in campsites. Blackwoods Campground had the only campsites left open. Misfortunately, we camped by a kid who desperately needed calming down who was "faster than Captain Underpants" on his bike. He liked to loudly boss his dog around, and when I saw him kick it, I had to tell him to knock it off and never do that again. I wonder who showed him that? Our other campground neighbor had a van with a generator that could have run a hotel, which fired up every

10 minutes or so and ran for 9 minutes. Were we being punished for never celebrating those holidays?

The park loop road was filled with pull-outs and parking for vistas and hikes. We started the day with Steve's favorite hike, "The Precipice", where it was often a boulder scramble except for an occasional blue painted stripe for guidance. At one point we had to pull ourselves straight up by steel bars drilled into boulders. Steve had to give my butt a boost when I stalled out. It's hell to be short.

As we drove to the next point we saw a foggy Atlantic Ocean with small islands dotted throughout as far as we could see, which wasn't far. We stopped at Thunder Hole where ocean water hit a slit, slipped under a cliff and spewed back out. Although the boulder and water seemed a gloomy shade of gray, my camera picked up the same colors as the brochure showed, with blues and coral showing colorfully.

We continued our loop to stop at Otter Point and Bubble Point.

One of the gathering areas was a restaurant by Jason's Pond. Nearby was the Gatehouse where early travelers by carriage were welcomed. It seemed that someone was staying upstairs; the window was slightly opened to the side and a curtain breezed gently and teasingly, so that tourists wondered at its history….and its present.

At our campsite we ate crab cakes we had bought in Farmington, which were second only to 119 Bistro in Longmont, CO.

The second day we thought we had a better idea of the time table we would need, so we left our campsite early to go to Jason's Pond to find a parking place. We rode bikes over Acadia's carriage roads, from Jason's Pond behind the Gatehouse to loop Eagle Lake past Bubble Pond, and returned to Jason's Pond. We crossed rock bridges where boulders and rock walls lined most of the paths. The roads were a uniform base, so riding was easy and enjoyable with a few hills. Very east coast!

On Desert Island we visited Cadillac Mountain and had clear vistas of the Atlantic with tour ships coming to shore.

Although there was a storm brewing, we traveled farther north in Maine on Hwy 1 Coastal. After being in Bar Harbor and Acadia National Park, the poverty we witnessed on Coastal 1 was disturbing. Many run down, storm beaten homes were for sale along with roadside shops and cottages that had formerly been rented. The turning leaves showed the most intense color we had seen, as if trying to make up for the depressing economy. We saw some vibrant patches of cranberries. We decided to find a place to stay a little earlier than usual, and we selected some tidy cottages above the "Million Dollar View" outside Houlton, but they, too, were for sale and empty.

When we were turned down twice at motels for having Ike along, we took a wrong turn and ended up on the interstate heading south. We were fooled by an attractive exterior on an outdated motel in Smyrna Falls, but were wooed by the powerful shower head. After 2 days at Acadia without showers, we took 2 showers each. The café that was on the motel grounds made up for the dated interior of our room: the food was divine with homemade everything.

We felt very accomplished regarding our goals as we began to retrace our route back to J. and N.'s in upstate New York.

The farms in Maine, New Hampshire and Vermont seemed to be too small to eke out a living. Rock clearing must have been an endless task. Some farms looked very tidy. Sometimes barns or shops were attached to the house. How convenient that would be for our farmer friends, especially the one who loved his arm chair!

Upon first entering Vermont, Route 2, we came across a fall fair in the college town of Woodstock; it looked as if it had drawn thousands. On the way back, it seemed almost as crowded with a constant flow of tourists. Both pass- throughs showed that it was beautifully decorated with flowering kale and mums, and it even had a covered bridge-the epitome of what one should expect to see in Vermont. We saw clever shops including "The Flannel Co".

On I-91 in Vermont the rock cliff sides shone as if they were black schist.

We stopped at Old Town to view their canoe outlet store. OSHA had caused them to show videos of the construction process instead of allowing tours, so we watched a video of our Otter kayak; it certainly wasn't the same as having a tour. We saw some $3,000 wooden canoes and some canoes with fiberglass exteriors and wooden interiors. When we went outside, there had been a wreck on the corner beside our truck. We thought that they had been gawking at our rig and hit each other. Steve had lots of compliments on the serviceability of his invention on the truck with steel sides that could fold up to contain our kayaks and camping gear, or fold down to create tables. We witnessed lots of stares and studying wherever we went.

We stopped to fill up with diesel in New Hampshire at the same place we had bought it on the way to Maine. The price had jumped from $2.15 to $2.22.

We stopped again at J. and N's and they seemed pleased and not too surprised to see us. We took them out for their anniversary dinner at the Algonquin. I had Fra Diavolo with giant clams and shrimp which would put our Colorado restaurants' shrimpy shrimp to deep shame.

After J. and N's we were on our homeward journey, but decided to visit Cooperstown. We both were bored by the Baseball Hall of Fame-45 minutes would have been quite enough. It was a very old town, founded by James Fennimore Cooper. We moved on to a farm museum where a few acres of stone buildings were picture worthy. We missed the tour which guided tourists through a farmer's life in the 1700's.

The golf course across from the farm was named Leatherstocking after Cooper's "Leatherstocking Tales."

We were to have Glimmerglass State Park nearly to ourselves that night. It was situated on a river where swimming and boating were allowed. There may have been 250 picnic tables for the summer crowd, along with a 3,000 square foot building for concession stands. We finally walked on a covered bridge. Within the park was an old mansion, open for tours, except for the time we were there!

I just had to visit Amish country, though it was out of the way, off the route. Pennsylvania-Steve's most hated state. There was far too much traffic. It looked as if Pennsylvanians had torn down all their sylvan areas to build highways. It was more like Transylvania to us.

We stayed in a campground in driving rain which called itself a "Resort in the heart of Pennsylvania Dutch country." Since the Amish left Germany for religious freedom, shouldn't they be called the Pennsylvania Deutsch?

We visited the new Cabela's in Hamburg. People spoke of it in worshipful tones. Cabela's had a "Deer Country" room devoted entirely to Boone and Crockett typical and non-typical antler point's ratings. The non-typicals looked like knife points or moose antlers, or hooves grown awry. The robot old-timer hunter looked real as he told his stories. It was eerie to watch his eyes and facial expressions: he seemed too human. I bought my sister Terry a rabbit and nylon hat.

The Lancaster area contained Amish and Mennonite towns with catchy, daring names like Bird-in-Hand and Intercourse. The weak history of the name adoption was a little unbelievable- they had seen them on a sign or on a bar front. Upon arrival in Bird-in-Hand, one of the town names printed in red on the map, we followed, in our diesel burning Dodge, two cute Amish kids in the back of a buggy, wearing black, who turned around and gave us a big, almost-practiced smile as if they wanted their picture taken. As we walked, an eleven-year-old boy scooted past us with one knee in his old wooden wagon while the other leg powered it. He easily guided it along a street with a narrow shoulder while modern traffic whizzed by. Weekends brought thousands of visitors, so they've been exposed to the outside world and traffic jams. As Steve asked him how he was, he replied that he was doing great.

"Pennsylvania's oldest hardware store" drew crowds, including us. It was like an old-fashioned McGuckin's Hardware store in Boulder with every item one could need as well as some decorations that were up to date. Steve bought a belt advertised as harness leather, while I bought my sister Joyce a wooden spoon…..made in France!

We joined the crowds for lunch at an Amish buffet where food was very like what Steve's granny would have cooked, including pork ribs and sauerkraut. We sat at the counter and a professional photographer sat beside us. He told me that he never took pictures of the Amish, because he felt it was an invasion of their privacy, but he would take pictures of their stores, buggies and way of life. Our Amish waitress didn't refuse the tip we left her, and in fact, seemed to look for it hungrily when she thought we had left without tipping.

Traffic following the map's red route crawled along, while Steve suffered. Finally, we had both had enough, and he took a short-cut off the loop route and drove by farms with buggies in their yards. These were in the wealthy looking farms as well, ones that looked somewhat modern. We followed a buggy on a 2-lane road and observed that all their buggy pulling horses were small with slender legs. We finally found a safe place to pass and found inside the hooded buggy an unbearded young man with a typical straw hat.

Another treasure we found by our short-cut was a farm machinery sales yard with small, horse-powered plows, planters and mowers with gearing to utilize hydraulics.

When we were finally free of weekend traffic, we traveled to Hershey where we stayed in a crusty campground. The town and factory would be ashamed if they knew how badly they were represented there, although there was a nice walk there, a good picnic ground and free wood for a fire- that is, free because we found it. The next morning we planned to take the factory tour and accidentally ended up at the elaborate Hershey Hotel for breakfast. The landscaping consisted of formal gardens, bountiful hanging baskets and colorful koi in their pools by their backyard fountain. Included was a golf course behind all the landscape.

The dining room was expansive with large windows decorated with stained glass foliage and birds within a type of filigree edging. Hungry, overweight people actively attacked the tables mounded with inviting, attractive food for their breakfast buffet. We were served coffee from a silver coffee pot, and had individual maple syrups with the Hershey label on it. Our butter was blended with cocoa in a floral shape.

Inside the factory, we entered a roller coaster type tramway. As we traveled in it, it turned us toward the screen or diorama we needed to see. When the description of the roasted almonds appeared, we were roasted under red lights. Steve was so impressed by our beauty that he bought our picture that had been taken while we were in the roller coaster.

It took most of the trip and a lifetime, but near Sigourney, Iowa, we saw pigs grazing in a field, not in a factory institution. We went to see Lyle Dumont's museum to see our friend, Jay Gould's Oliver tractor that Lyle had beautifully and perfectly restored, and view the other old, restored Oliver or John Deere tractors, mowers and engines. The prize for the strangest looking were orchard and high crop tractors. They sat up so high that we could practically walk under them, a little hunched. The orchard tractors had fenders around the wheels all the way down to protect them. The corn cutting tractors were positively alien-like.

Steve was so ready to go home that he drove into the night in a raging rain storm complete with an electric light show. Finally, we found a motel. When we were ready to unload the camper items into the motel room in Grinell, Iowa, Ike and I ran toward the room, but I felt that the lightening pushed us back toward the motel. Steve yelled over the noise to, "Get in!" When we climbed back into the truck, he asked what I was doing there......he had meant for us to get into the room! Later, when the storm calmed a little, we went out. Ike finally used her time well, and peed almost instantly.

On our way back we traveled through Grand Island, Omaha and Lincoln, cities we rarely pass through. I can more greatly appreciate Steve's mom's friend, Dick, and his travel to Boulder so often; it was a lengthy day's journey for an older man.

Though the last few days of the trip were tunnel-visioned with the goal of going home, we plan to do the trip again, cross country. Our senses were filled, and our appreciation of true friendships were reawakened as we picked up where we left off.

Acknowledgements

My family has been so supportive in this endeavor, hardly ever criticizing my work, thus we see the result! My sisters, Joyce Baker and Terry Wood, and my nephew Abe Wood, have carried me along, encouraging me. My cousin, Sandi Kristen Olsen, and her beautiful art work appear as a cover picture of the Flatirons in Boulder, as well as my late husband, Steve's portrait in his hip boots, a quintessential look of his. The trout farm couldn't have persisted without his hard work and brilliance. I thank him deeply for letting me share our lives together. A few good friends, Nancy Anderson and Jan Gray, busy ladies, took a little time out to critique a bit of writing, Deborah Wynne, a published writer herself, gave me tips, sent me books and helped me with ideas of how to even begin. Vicki Kinzie, another friend and published writer gave me some sage advice. Dominic Del Bone, my sister Terry's friend, was dragged into the foray at times and offered insightful comments.

My informal writing class, created and gently led by my attorney, Biff Warren, as well as the participants with opinions and guidance. Anne Moses and Jan Swanson, voracious readers, gave me valuable insights for revisions. Anne took work home to analyze and critique intensely, writing drafts of suggestions.

I want to thank my late parents for giving me a working brain and mostly giving me my way when I wanted to do something!

About the Author

Born in the far northeastern Colorado town of Holyoke, Peggy moved with her family to Weld County where her parents were wheat farmers. When she married Steve, they lived in Boulder, where Steve, his father and brother raised trout to stock in private ponds and streams. A friend's husband described Peggy as being a combination of Boulder and Weld County, which combined a compliment with a slight insult; however, she agreed with his description. With degrees from the University of Northern Colorado and a Master's degree from CU in Boulder, she taught reading to high school and middle schoolers in the mainly Italian and Hispanic town of Frederick, CO. She's excited to publish since it took her a lifetime to experience and write the stories. She hopes her stories don't insult anyone; she has few filters!

Facebook: Peggy Cline
pcline48@gmail.com